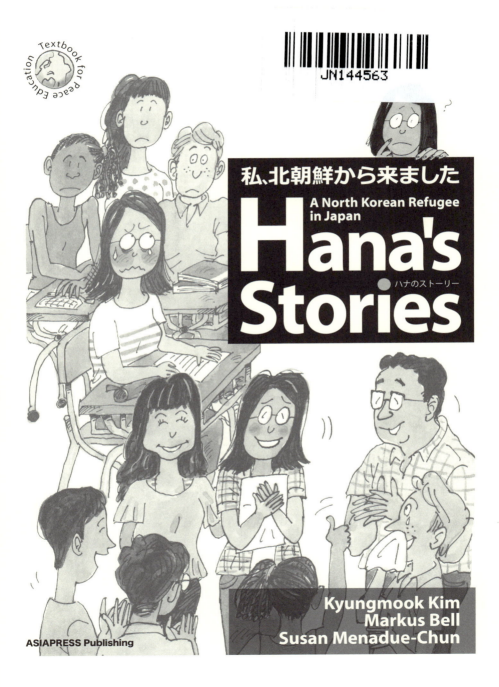

ASIAPRESS International Osaka Office

Sanukaito BLDG 303, 1-2-3

Ukita, Kita, OSAKA, #530-0021,

JAPAN

TEL+FAX +81-6-6373-2444

osaka@asiapress.org

Copyright © 2016 ASIAPRESS

All rights reserved.

Published 2016

Japanese-English, Bilingual Textbook for Peace Education

A North Korean Refugee in Japan——Hana's Stories

Authors: Kyungmook Kim, Markus Bell, and Susan Menadue-Chun

Publisher: ISHIMARU Jiro

Illustrator: Chung In-kyung

Book Design: HAYASHI Mariko

ISBN 978-4-904399-11-8

Printed in Japan on acid-free paper

Prologue

This textbook was originally written in English and then translated into Japanese as accurately as possible. Some expressions that did not translate well were changed or omitted. It is the product of a two-year research project, from November 2012 until October 2014, and was generously supported by the Toyota Foundation (Research Material No. D12-R-0657-*The Ideal and the Reality of Overseas North Korean Defectors: From the Perspective of Transnational Networks and Border Controls*).

This international research project looked at the phenomenon of North Korean *re-migrants:* North Korean refugees who, after temporarily settling in the Republic of Korea (South Korea), have left and settled in a third country – Australia, Japan, North America or in Europe. More specifically, this project focused on North Korean re-migrants living in Australia and Japan.

Firstly, this research project represented a new approach to studying the phenomenon of North Korean refugees: those migrating to South Korea and then re-migrating. Clearly, the government of South Korea makes great efforts in facilitating the settlement process of these individuals and, in comparison to the policies of other refugee-receiving nations, the institutions in place in South Korea are robust and continuously improving. Nevertheless, the fact that North Koreans continue to re-migrate from South Korea to Europe, North America or other destinations is enough to suggest that there remains room for improvement. Improvements can be made in terms of the current policies for receiving these individuals in South Korea, for understanding the motivations for leaving, and in learning more about what happens to those who move to third countries. It is important to consider that the psychological, social and cultural conflict experienced by those who re-migrate could have greater significance to contemporary life in Northeast Asia than the division of the Korean peninsula itself.

There are a variety of methods through which we can tackle this issue. This research project has chosen to create educational materials and employ already existing educational institutions to teach this subject. This is the starting point from which the authors believe a solution for such an emotional and complicated problem lies – from individuals with some distance from the intricate geo-politics of Northeast Asia.

Ultimately, however, the answers to problems of such magnitude do not lie inside the covers of this textbook. Rather, the authors hope that the materials and exercises therein will offer the reader something to help them rethink and question what they might already have strong opinions about. It is expected that this text will encourage new questions, and offer fresh challenges to both the student and the teacher. Further, it is hoped that conversations, ideas and opinions prompted by stories in this book will assist in considering issues of cultural difference, mutual understanding and the importance of coexistence. Furthermore, this book uses "Global English" otherwise known as "World Englishes." This is a new concept, not confined to only British and American English.

A vague sympathy for North Korean refugees, or refugees anywhere, for that matter, will not help their situation, nor will it contribute to solving any of the problems associated with their plight. In our everyday lives, when we have questions about someone or something, there are times when it is too difficult to simply voice our curiosities. If we are curious about people who have left North Korea, sometimes it can be difficult to know what to ask or how to ask them our questions. This book was developed and based on the aforementioned problems and cannot answer all the questions associated with North Korean refugees and re-migration. However, it is my hope that it will bring attention to part of this phenomenon and start a dialogue. If more and more people begin to ask questions, to understand cultural differences and the variation within our societies, I have no doubt that our shared living spaces will become more peaceful and rays of sunshine will creep into even the darkest of corners.

The authors hope that this book can be used as a starting point for such actions. The authors wish to end this prologue by thanking all those who kindly contributed towards the creation of this textbook. Especially, the authors wish to thank the Chukyo University and fellow researchers for the partial funds used from the "2015 Chukyo University Special Research Grant / Joint Research B (Representative: Professor KAZAMA Takashi)," for this project.

        KIM Kyungmook Ph.D.
        Professor of Peace Studies, Chukyo University

The Global Citizens' School

In Hana's stories, the fictional "Global Citizens' School" (GCS) was created in 2007, by a motivated group of educators, academics and business people living in Japan and South Korea. The individuals who contributed to creating the GCS envisioned an educational institute situated 'beyond borders.' This would be a place allowing students to imagine themselves as citizens of the world, where their nationality and the fact that the school is located in Japan would be of less importance than their dreams for the future and the relationships they build within the school.

For a long time, in Japan, ethnic Korean schools have been cast as either North or South Korean, while Japanese schools were unequivocally Japanese. Given the shared history of Japan and the two Koreas, the GCS was conceived as a space where divisive history would be transcended. The focus on teaching collective history from a Japanese, Korean and international perspective, would facilitate in overcoming difference and helping students find their place in the global community, rather than as only Japanese or Korean or *Zainichi*.

The GCS that the fictional character, Hana, attends is located on the outskirts of Osaka. The community donated the funds required to start the school, with local Japanese and *Zainichi* Korean business people providing the bulk of what was needed. Although the school is small, teachers and students come from many different countries, underlining the aspirations of the school to be a global space.

The GCS is a work in progress and by no means entirely free from the political and historical issues which continue to prevent a conciliation of different nationalities in Northeast Asia. Nevertheless, even as an aspirational project, it is self-supporting and not required to bow to the wishes of either the Japanese or Korean government. Therefore, it stands as an example of grassroots, transnational co-operation, created by people who understand that in order for people everywhere to live in peace, mutual understanding and an ability to live outside one's borders is first required.

Contents

Prologue KIM Kyungmook Ph.D. Professor of Peace Studies, Chukyo University 3

The Global Citizens' School 6

Character Profiles 8

Case study 1 **A New Start at the Global Citizens' School** 10

Case study 2 **Hana Starts a Blog** 12

Case study 3 **Yumi's Secret** 14

Case study 4 **The Conditions for Being a National Representative** 18

Case study 5 **The Trouble with History** 22

Case study 6 **Hana Visits an Ethnic Korean School** 24

Case study 7 **Hate Crimes** 27

Case study 8 **Mr. Yamashita Almost Lets the Cat Out of the Bag** 30

Case study 9 **Biting Off More than You Can Chew** 34

Case study 10 **Does *Hankuk-saram* Mean Korean?** 37

Case study 11 **Hana Visits 'Nishi Nihon Detention Centre'** 41

Case study 12 **Hana and Aaron Go to the Movies** 45

Case study 13 **Hana Writes a Letter Home** 47

Case study 14 **Is Reunification Necessary?** 51

Case study 15 **The New Girl: What is She?** 54

Case study 16 **Hana's Big Secret** 57

Epilogue Markus Bell The Australian National University 62

Character Profiles © Chung In-kyung

Hana

Hana is a complicated character and she feels this herself. She was born and brought up in North Korea. Her parents and grandparents migrated to North Korea from Japan during the repatriation project that took place from 1959-1984. When she was 15 years old her parents, worried about Hana's future in North Korea, organized for her to leave for China. They hoped she would be able to find a brighter future over the border. Conditions in China, however, were little better for her and she soon realised that she could not return to North Korea without risking her life and the lives of her family members. With the help of an NGO in Japan she arrived in Osaka just after her 17th birthday. The NGO helped prove her family is *Zainichi* Korean and this was enough to convince the Japanese government to accept her in Japan. She worked part time and went to night school to study Japanese and English, and to try to catch up with her education.

Hana studied hard at the night school and, with the help of a Japanese NGO, she was invited to attend a special school on the outskirts of the city. The GCS is less an international school than it is an aspirational project, aiming to create 'young people without borders.' As a result, Hana's classmates come from all over the world. At 19 years old, Hana is older than all of her classmates, a fact she keeps a secret. This is not the only secret Hana hides. Not wanting to shock her new classmates and aware of the stigma attached to anything related to North Korea, Hana tells people she is from South Korea. How long she will be able to keep her secret is yet to be seen.

Yumi

Yumi is a Japanese student of Korean descent. She has struggled with her Korean identity and chosen to keep her Korean roots a secret. In her Japanese high school she worried that people would discover her secret. It was with this in mind her parents decided to move her to the GCS in the hope that she would identify herself as a global citizen and not someone defined by a Japanese passport.

Hyang-mi

Hyang-mi is Hana's friend. She attends the local ethnic Korean school. She is a self-assured *Zainichi* Korean who speaks openly about the bond she feels for her 'fatherland,' North Korea, and the strong connection with other members of the *Zainichi* Korean community. Outside of school, however, she speaks in Japanese and wears the latest Japanese fashions, appearing to be like any other young Japanese person.

In-ho

In-ho is a third generation *Zainichi* Korean. He is a big soccer fan and particularly keen on well-known *Zainichi* player, Jung Tae-Se.

Aaron

Aaron is Hana's classmate and her first western friend. His background is almost as complicated as Hana's; he was born in Northern Ireland and his family is Catholic. During difficult times in Ireland his family migrated to Canada and Aaron now holds Canadian and United Kingdom citizenship. He has come to the GCS as an exchange student and is making the most of his year, studying Japanese and getting to know what goes on with his multi-cultural classmates.

Mr. Yamashita

Mr. Yamashita is Hana's homeroom teacher, as well as being a history teacher. He is Japanese and has been teaching at the GCS since it was established in 2007. Mr. Yamashita is one of the few people who knows Hana's secret but does not give her any special treatment because of it. Despite coming across as quite strict, Mr. Yamashita has a heart of gold and is keen to help his students develop as 'global citizens.'

Takuya

Takuya is Hana's Japanese classmate. He was born in Osaka. He graduated from both a Japanese primary school and junior high school. He entered the GCS from high school. This was a decision made by his parents because they felt it would benefit Takuya to be educated as a global citizen. Takuya is a cheeky, happy-go-lucky boy and sometimes gets in trouble with his classmates.

Mariko/Tina

Mariko/Tina is new to the GCS. As a new arrival, with her unusual style and confident manner, she attracts a lot of attention. Mariko/Tina's father is Japanese American and her mother is Korean American. Because of her father's job she has travelled a lot and grown up all over the world. She uses Mariko as her Japanese name and Tina as her English name.

Junho and Chul

Junho and Chul are South Korean overseas students studying at the GCS. They are co-representatives of the South Korean Students' Association at the school. The association holds fortnightly meetings, during which they discuss matters of Korean culture and history.

Case study 1
A New Start at the Global Citizens' School

Hana stepped off the bus that had taken her from the train station to the front of her new school. As she walked through the gates that opened up to the soccer field she glanced at the sign on the side of the school:

"Global Citizens' School," she read out loud to herself.

"What in the world does that mean?"

She did not have any time to contemplate this further as from out of one of the white washed buildings emerged a tall, bespectacled man walking directly towards her and apparently in quite a hurry.

"Hana? Hana Lee?" He called out, before offering Hana his outstretched hand.

"Hello there, Hana. My name is Mr. Yamashita. I will be your homeroom teacher here at the GCS," he continued, not waiting for Hana to reply.

"Please follow me."

Hana had to skip to keep up with Mr. Yamashita as she followed him back into the building and up the stairs. The walls of the corridors were covered with posters showing school trips: "Volunteering in the Philippines," one was titled. "Raising Money for Schools in Cambodia," another read. Mr. Yamashita rounded the corner into a classroom and Hana followed him in.

"Welcome, Hana. This will be your homeroom for the next year. Your seat is marked with your name. I must say, I'm excited to have a student from North Korea," Mr. Yamashita smiled warmly.

"Actually," Hana hesitated.

"Please don't tell people I'm from North Korea."

"Hmm. Are you sure about that?" Mr. Yamashita asked, a little taken aback.

"I just think it's better that way. I'd be more comfortable if people think I'm from South Korea. I know what most people think about North Korea and I want to make things simple," explained Hana.

"Well. If that's how you feel then I'll keep your secret, Hana. But I want you to know that this is a school where a person's identity isn't defined by where they come from. At the GCS, a person's character speaks louder than their citizenship or ethnicity."

"I understand, Mr. Yamashita. Thank you. I'm just not ready yet," replied Hana.

"Your secret is safe with me, Hana. Let's help you settle in and make some new friends," reassured Mr. Yamashita again.

"How are you at history?" he asked.

"I'm a big fan of weekly history tests."

"Oh dear," responded Hana.

"This could be a long year."

Keyword global citizen, nationality, ethnicity, defector.

Discussion Questions
- ☐ Why might Hana want to keep her background a secret from her classmates?
- ☐ What does Mr. Yamashita mean when he tells Hana that a person's character is more important than their citizenship or ethnicity?

Activities

In groups of 2-3 consider how many identities you have and how you might organize them. For example, family identity, local identity, gender identity.

Which of your identities are most important to you and why?

Case study 2
Hana Starts a Blog

It was another rainy day in Osaka and Hana was feeling reluctant to get out of bed. Each time the alarm went off she would slam her hand down on the button and wriggle further under the covers. Finally, after much procrastinating, she pulled back the sheets and shuffled over to the computer to check her emails.

No messages!

"That makes things easy," she said to herself, under her breath, beginning to scroll through the updates her friends had posted on their "Friendbook" wall.

"It's all so dull," she muttered, gliding past another picture of her friend's breakfast.

"I bet I could write a much better update."

She paused, catching her reflection for a moment in the dark edges of the computer screen. In recent days, she had been feeling anxious. The secrets she was harbouring had started to weigh heavy on her, but she had no one to confide in.

"I bet I could write a whole blog with some of the stories I have, the story of a North Korean refugee in Japan. Only, I'd have to do it in secret, using a pseudonym," she exclaimed.

Hana was excited, but at the same time worried that her classmates might get to know her shocking story.

"I'm going to do it," she exclaimed, resolutely.

"I'm going to start a blog telling my stories."

Without waiting to shower or change out of her pyjamas, Hana took just moments to find a free blog site. With the rain still coming down outside, she entered her details and started designing the layout of her new blog.

"And last, but not least, the blog itself."

Hana could feel her heart beating harder as she opened up the first page of her blog and clicked delicately on the *New Draft* option. Up popped an empty white page, unblemished aside from the cursor that now waited impatiently for its first command. Closing her eyes, Hana moved her fingers over the keyboard and, taking a deep breath, began to type:

"I am a North Korean refugee living in Japan. My life wasn't that different from anyone else's. I'd study at school during the day and play with my friends every chance I got. Then, one day, everything changed and I had to leave my friends, family and country behind…"

Keyword social media, life story, communication.

Discussion Questions
☐ What are the advantages of new digital media for people like Hana, who have a story to tell but don't know how to tell it?
☐ What are the risks involved in blogging?

Activities

In groups of 2-3 people, discuss how you will design and start your own blog.

Decide on the main theme of the blog and think of common interests in the group, perhaps sports, music or food, and set a schedule for how often you will update your blog.

Decide who will be in charge of visuals, who will write the homepage introduction and who will write the self-introduction page. Think of this as a semester project that you can continue later.

Case study 3
Yumi's Secret

When Hana started at her new school her homeroom teacher, Mr. Yamashita, suggested she buddy up with a Japanese student, Yumi.

"Hi, Hana. You look a bit nervous. Why don't we go out for dinner to get to know each other?" Yumi suggested.

Hana agreed and that evening Yumi took her to a Korean barbeque restaurant.

"I thought this might be something familiar to you," Yumi said, turning over the sizzling pieces of beef with a pair of tongs.

"This is wonderful, Yumi," replied Hana.

"I hardly ever eat as well as this," Hana blushed.

"I want to welcome you to our school," Yumi said.

"So tonight it's on me."

"Oh! Gosh. That's not necessary," replied Hana, feeling a little overwhelmed.

"Don't worry about it. I'm friends with the owner," smiled Yumi.

Over the following months, Hana and Yumi spent a lot of time together, becoming close friends. They shared a passion for *AKB 48* and spent hours improving their English together, chatting over their favourite fashion magazine *Seventeen*, and what their horoscope said about boys. In spite of their strong friendship, Hana found it curious that Yumi didn't want to talk about her family. She always seemed so private.

Then, one day in class, Aaron whispered to Hana,

"Junho and Chul were out for dinner in a Korean restaurant last night and they saw Yumi's parents working there. They had met Yumi's parents at the school festival earlier that year. They think Yumi is Korean."

Hana was not sure what to think of this.

"Why wouldn't she tell me if she is Korean?" pondered Hana.

Aaron added more to the speculation, "We all know that Yumi's father is a successful businessman. I heard that he owns a chain of over 30 barbeque restaurants."

Hana thought back to her dinner with Yumi and remembered how generous the staff had been with them both.

"Could that have been Yumi's parents' restaurant?"

Hana thought about her own family's background; the stories she had heard from her grandmother about Japan, and their life as *Zainichi* Koreans. Still, she didn't feel she could be direct and ask her friend what was going on. She wondered if Yumi's shyness had something to do with her "secret identity." Her curiosity piqued, Hana decided to ask Mr. Yamashita about *Zainichi* Koreans.

"Well, Hana, I think you should choose this topic as your presentation project and learn more about the history of *Zainichi* Koreans and your family history," Mr. Yamashita said.

"*Zainichi* Koreans live in Japan as a consequence of Japan's colonization of Korea. During that time many Koreans migrated from impoverished Korea and resettled in Japan," he explained.

"After 1945, a large number of Koreans returned to their homeland but about 600,000 people stayed in Japan. Since then Koreans in Japan were treated as foreigners and discriminated against by Japanese. Of these *Zainichi* Koreans, many chose to use a Japanese alias and hide anything that might give away their Korean background. You know, you might want to look into this further," he added.

Hana was surprised and felt sorry that Yumi had to hide her identity. Wanting to learn more, she took the subway to Korea town, in Tsuruhashi. Wandering through Tsuruhashi, Hana suddenly felt very comfortable. Many of the brightly lit signs were written in both Korean and Japanese. Shop assistants called out to customers in both languages and restaurants were selling kimchee and sweet meats.

"So this is zero ground of the *Zainichi* Korean community," she thought to herself.

Hana understood that despite being a naturalized Japanese, Yumi's se-

cret was likely a coping mechanism for handling her identity conflict and preventing possible discrimination. Heading back home she started thinking about her own secrets. Would she ever be able to open up to her friends?

Keyword naturalization, passing for, identity, ethnicity, citizenship.

Activities

In groups of 2-4 discuss and record your answers to the following:

☐ What does it mean to hide one's identity?

☐ Why do you think Yumi still feels the need to pass for Japanese, even though she now attends an international school?

☐ Imagine you are Hana, would you talk directly to Yumi and tell her you know her secret? What would you say?

☐ Can you think of any other groups of people in Japan or in other countries who experience a similar identity conflict as Yumi?

Case study 4
The Conditions for Being a National Representative

The FIFA World Cup was well under way and Hana's school had gone soccer crazy. Every lunch break saw Hana's classmates trading facts about the superstars and making predictions on which team would make the final sixteen. Today's lunch break was no different as In-ho, Junho, and Aaron had booked the seminar room and were chatting about their favourite players.

In-ho was a big fan of Jung Tae-Se.

"There's nothing I don't know about him. One day, I'm going to be just like him," In-ho told the group, excitedly.

"Sorry, In-ho. But who is this guy, Jung Tae-se?" asked Aaron, a little puzzled. "I thought I knew all the famous players."

"Really? You don't know him? Okay. Well, Jung Tae-Se is a third generation *Zainichi* Korean. He was born and raised in Japan, and went to an ethnic Korean school while holding South Korean citizenship. As a professional soccer player, he played in the J-league in Japan, the K-league in South Korea, and the *Bundesliga* in Germany. One of the reasons he's so famous is because he played in the 2010 FIFA World Cup as a representative of North Korea."

As he spoke, In-ho's eyes lit up and he became animated with the chance to tell someone about his hero.

"You know, I'm also third generation *Zainichi* Korean and Jung's a great role model for people like me. If I train hard enough I could also represent South Korea or Japan. I don't want to play for North Korea, but I understand Jung's situation as a *Zainichi*."

Junho, a South Korean student, seemed confused by In-ho's statements. Scratching his head, he pondered,

"It seems to me that Jung is merely opportunistic. I think if he has South Korean nationality, then he should only be allowed to represent South Korea. I know he's your hero, In-ho, but it's hardly conventional for him to have played in Japan, South Korea and even in Germany during his football career, and then represented North Korea without trying to become a member of the

South Korean national team. My father taught me that one's nationality is like destiny, it can't be changed like a pair of old socks. Especially for Koreans, we have the shame of colonial history behind us, which should be a motivator to take extra pride in your country."

"You know guys," interrupted Aaron, "I'm also from a country that has experienced colonization and division. A lot of countries have endured this kind of hardship and it seems to me that nationality is less important than how you feel personally about yourself and your country or countries. If Jung can play these different roles then why not let him? If he's a great soccer player then that will shine through whichever uniform he wears. I know that if I ever have the chance to represent the Northern Ireland or Canada I'll take whatever comes my way."

The group returned to discussing the games that had recently been played agreeing, at least for now, that the game was more important than the politics. Uncertain where she stood on the matter, Hana pondered what nationality, ethnicity and citizenship meant. Where did she fit in? Was she South Korean? North Korean? Could she even be *Zainichi*?

Keyword ethnicity, nationality, opportunism, home.

Discussion Questions

☐ After hearing the various opinions of the discussion regarding nationality and identity, whose opinion is most persuasive to you?

☐ In your opinion, which country should Jung Tae-Se represent and which should he not be allowed to, if any?

☐ Do you find it acceptable to be able to change one's nationality in order to participate in sporting events?

Activities

In groups of 2-4 discuss and record your answers to the following:

In order to explore how identity goes beyond the colour of the passport you hold, make up a list of objects, symbols and imagery that you feel most accurately represents who you are. You should consider things such as race, religion, gender, language and family, and the effect of these things in shaping a person's identity.

Once you have finished making the list, have one member of your group, report back your findings and discuss these with the larger group. Why did you choose these symbols? On reviewing them, are there any you would not choose next time? Are there any you would add to the list?

Case study 5
The Trouble with History

"Alright everyone! Do you know what today is?"

Mr. Yamashita called out to the startled students.

"It's surprise test day! That's right everybody, you'd better have your thinking caps on because I've prepared 20 short answer questions on Japanese history for you all."

The students let out a collective groan, but Mr. Yamashita was not finished.

"Oh, and don't worry Hana, I've even included some questions on Japan-Korea issues. They should be easy for you."

Hana felt particularly depressed at the prospect of failing another one of Yamashita's pop quizzes. Glancing over, Yumi noticed Hana's expression.

"Hana, are you alright?"

"You know I hate history, Yumi. I've just arrived in Japan so it's a struggle to take it all in. And a Monday morning history quiz just seems extra cruel," replied Hana, now slumped over her desk in resignation.

"It's always the same: the teacher throws questions at us and constantly seems to pick on me. I never get any of them right and I feel like a fool," she added.

"I know what you mean," Yumi reflected.

"It's a pity that you struggle with this just because you're from South Korea. History is about perspective, right? The two Koreas teach different versions of history. The cause of the Korean War is just one example of many."

"That's true. The Japanese history I learnt before coming here was full of negative things about Japan. Mainly about Japanese colonization. Neither neutrality nor fairness can be applied in this. It's easily biased," said Hana, contemplatively.

"If it makes you feel any better, history is my worst subject, too. But my parents always tell me that it's all fiction anyway, so I shouldn't worry about it. They believe that in the national history of each country lie the seeds for future conflict. Seriously, my father always tries to teach me about the shared aspects of Asian history; local, family history at the grassroots level."

Hana smiled at Yumi. The idea that history is a made-up story appealed to her. Unfortunately it wouldn't save her from Mr. Yamashita's obsession with surprise testing. If only they were given tests on her hometown's history, or on her family history, she thought. She would show them she was not so ignorant. Another Monday and another chance to fail a Japanese history test. She hated history class.

Keyword

national history, local history, family history, minority history, facts, fiction.

Discussion Questions

☐ What do you think a common Asian history would look like?

☐ How might the history of minority groups be different from the majority group?

☐ What is the purpose of history for a community or a family? Is it possible to have competing histories in the same community or family?

☐ To what extent is history 'true' or 'made up'? Give reasons to support your view.

Case study 6
Hana Visits an Ethnic Korean School

Hana was bubbling with excitement; she had made her first friend outside of school and to her delight her new friend, Hyang-mi, was a third generation *Zainichi* Korean. They had met at an event organized by a Japanese NGO for students at international schools.

"I was born in Japan and I've lived here my whole life, but I feel like the Korean peninsula is my homeland. That's why I'm still *Chosenseki*," Hyang-mi confidently told Hana, using fluent Korean.

Her honesty about what is considered an off-limit topic in Japan astonished Hana.

"What do you think about North Korea?" asked Hana, tentatively.

"Well, the government often seems to be in some kind of trouble," replied Hyang-mi.

"But I regard the two Koreas as my homeland. Actually," continued Hyang-mi.

"My school is having an open day this Sunday. Would you like to go with me?"

At first Hana hesitated to visit a school openly identifying with North Korea. It was a little too close to the troubles she had left behind. What if people found out that she is from the North? Hyang-mi seemed to be very friendly, however, and Hana's curiosity overcame her anxiety.

The next Sunday, Hyang-mi, dressed in her black *chogori* school uniform, waited for Hana at the school gate. Hana's apprehension subsided at the sight of visitors from the local Japanese school. The visitors were speaking in Japanese, while school students, preoccupied with their preparations, were speaking in Korean. Hana felt impressed at the multicultural atmosphere and her nerves began to settle. Ushering the guests inside, students greeted each visitor with a warm smile and an *"Annyeonghashimnika?"*

Hyang-mi led Hana to her seat and the concert began. The junior and high school students played traditional Korean orchestral instruments, while others sang and danced. The great pride they took in their performance suggested they had invested many hours of practice to perfect their skills. Hana was impressed. The songs and dances reminded her of her own schooldays in North Korea. The similarities made her feel both homesick and uncomfortable.

"What do you think, Hana?" asked Hyang-mi.

"It's lovely," replied Hana, a little uncertain of what it was she was seeing. "Everyone seems very supportive. Look!"

She gestured to a group of women dancing at the foot of the stage.

"Even the parents are getting into the spirit."

In the afternoon, the students returned to their classes and visitors wandered around experiencing '*A day in the life*' at an ethnic Korean school. Glancing around, Hana felt mixed feelings when she saw the many posters and pictures expressing the students' ethnic identity and connection to the North.

"It seems like there are some North Korean styles expressed," she cautiously probed.

"Well, yes. North Korea has always played a very important role supporting our schools, Hana. As I said to you, we regard both South Korea and North Korea as our homeland. That is a common understanding for people who go to *Chosun hakkyo*." "It's just, um, surprising," stammered Hana.

Changing the subject she asked, "Do they use Korean in classes here?"

"That's right. Usually Japanese is for outside of school. And we also learn English," replied Hyang-mi, leading Hana back out of the classroom and into the corridor.

At the end of the day the principal, Mr. Kim, assembled the guests and thanked everyone for visiting. In his talk he described the financial difficulties the school was facing. In particular, the troubled Japan-North Korea relationship had resulted in cuts in budgetary subsidies.

"Through positive community engagement, like today, we can all help in changing negative social attitudes," Mr. Kim encouraged, bowing deeply to the visitors.

"Hyang-mi, that was something special for me," said Hana, as they left the school at the end of the day.

"I'm glad you enjoyed it. I wish more people would be as open minded as you. I was proud to show around a visitor from South Korea," she replied, giving Hana a hug.

Hana stayed silent.

"You're very quiet Hana," she noticed.

"I had a great time. Let's hang out again soon," Hana smiled, realising this was not the time nor place for telling Hyang-mi her secret.

Arriving at home, Hana looked back on the day. She was again gripped by feelings of anxiousness.

Keyword

Korean language, multiculturalism, ethnic education, minorities in Japan.

Activities

In groups of 2-4 discuss and record your answers to the following:

☐ What do you know about ethnic Korean schools in Japan? What are your impressions of these schools?

☐ Why do you think the Japanese government does not give funding to ethnic Korean schools?

☐ Do you think ethnic education is important? Why or why not?

☐ What do you think Hana learned from her visit to the ethnic Korean school? Would you be interested in visiting such a school?

Case study 7
Hate Crimes

As with every morning, the first thing that Hana did when she woke up was to turn on her computer and skim through the comments on her blog stories. The number of visitors to her site was increasing day by day. Hana never forgot to make multiple checks, before and after uploading her stories, fearful that someone might figure out the identity of the author.

Scrolling down to the comments at the end of her latest posting, Hana suddenly felt the blood drain from her face.

"What on earth is this?" she said to herself, her eyes widening.

"DEATH TO KOREANS!"
"NO PLACE FOR NORTH KOREANS!"
"GO HOME FOREIGNERS! WE DON'T WANT CRIMINALS HERE!"
"JAPANESE ONLY!"

Screamed the message.
Hana was shocked and reeled back in her chair.
"How? What is this?" she stammered.

Her hands were trembling. Still unsure about what she was looking at, Hana realised she was late for school. Changing her clothes, she dashed out the door to meet Hyang-mi.

Although Hana and her new friend, Hyang-mi, go to different schools, for the past few weeks they had been walking together in the mornings. The two had become close friends, but Hana was still curious about Hyang-mi's appearance, each morning they met. She never turned up wearing her *chogori* school uniform. Instead she would meet Hana in an ordinary school uniform – a short plaid skirt, blazer and a necktie.

"May I ask you a question, Hyang-mi?"
Hyang-mi smiled and nodded her head.
"I don't know how to ask this but, is hate crime the reason you don't

wear a *chogori* uniform to school?"

A little surprised, Hyang-mi explained,

"This is what we call our second uniform, and you are right, it has a sad story behind it," replied Hyang-mi, her eyes fixed on the sidewalk in front of her.

"Can you tell me the story, if you don't mind?" asked Hana.

"To put it simply, I feel really anxious about wearing the *chima chogori*," replied Hyang-mi.

"In the past the *chogori* identified us as Koreans and there was a risk we could be the targets of hate crimes. So, for our personal safety, we wear a Japanese style uniform to school and change into the *chogori* when we arrive."

As they approached the gates of the Korean school, Hyang-mi described how, in the past, there were nationwide reports of female Korean high school students being attacked and having their *chogori* uniform slashed.

"Hyang-mi," Hana exclaimed.

"I think I may have stumbled across some things like that online."

Hana explained about the messages she had received and how shocked she had been. Hyang-mi did not seem so surprised.

She confirmed, "It sounds like hate speech, Hana. I'm really not sure there's anything you can do about it. It's a pity, but in every country there are narrow minded people."

Hana was confused. In fact the whole thing sounded bizarre. How could this happen in a constitutional country like Japan? Realising they were approaching Hyang-mi's school, the girls said goodbye and Hana continued to the GCS.

Keyword hate crime, hate speech, discrimination, xenophobia.

Activities

In groups of 2-4 discuss and record your answers to the following:

☐ *Zainichi* Koreans are Japan's oldest foreign minority. Why do you think they are still targeted in hate crimes?

☐ Should the government stop hate crimes? What do you think they could do to stop these things happening?

Case study 8
Mr. Yamashita Almost Lets the Cat Out of the Bag

Hana was having a difficult day at school. She had forgotten to bring her homework, leading to another run-in with her homeroom teacher, Mr. Yamashita, and she was feeling stressed about the upcoming class trip to South Korea.

Her friend, Aaron, was trying to cheer her up,

"Don't worry, Hana. I think Mr. Yamashita is tough on everyone. And we can do the homework together at lunchtime. It's no problem."

"Thanks Aaron. That's very kind of you," smiled Hana.

"That's what friends are for. Anyway, I thought you would be excited about going to South Korea this summer."

"Well, not really. It's complicated," Hana replied.

She was worried about the up-coming field trip to South Korea. Since her arrival, she had been telling people her hometown is in South Korea and now she realised there was a high chance her secret would be exposed.

"Ha! You sound like me. I hope you can be a free tour guide for me when we go," joked Aaron.

After taking a few deep breaths, Hana felt a little better. Since she had started at the GCS she had not made many friends, but the friends she had made, like Aaron, were very kind. The call to order from Mr. Yamashita interrupted her thoughts.

"Okay everybody. I want you all to remember we have a trip to the museum coming up this weekend. You all need to prepare your bento boxes and the worksheet I gave you. Also, you have to get there yourself so don't be late. Hana, I guess you need help with the subway? By the way, have you ever tried the Pyongyang subway?"

Hana froze. Her classmates fell silent.

"Er, er," she tried to speak.

She felt as if her classmates were staring at her and whispering behind her back.

"No. Of course I don't need help. I can use a subway. I take the subway all the time here in Japan. And I guess I can ride the Pyongyang subway when

reunification happens. But until then…," she trailed off.

One of her classmates started to snigger and Mr. Yamashita realised his mistake.

"Ah. Yes. How silly of me. Let's hope we can all try the Pyongyang subway on a future field trip."

Hana's face went bright red. She tried to smile but nothing happened. This was too close. Mr. Yamashita knew her secret and had almost let the cat out of the bag. For the rest of the day Hana did not talk to anyone, worried her classmates might ask what Mr. Yamashita had meant – "Have you tried Pyongyang subways before?"

Realising she needed to cool off, as soon as school finished Hana took the bus to her favourite Korean restaurant. The owner, Mrs. Lee, was *Zainichi* Korean and could speak Korean well. She had met Hana through an NGO in which she volunteered, helping returnees from North Korea. Over time, she had become a close friend to Hana.

"Mrs. Lee," called Hana, taking a seat at the window.

"I've had a tough day and I need some of your best *bibimbap*, please."

"Coming right up," replied Mrs. Lee.

"You do look troubled. What's wrong, Hana?" she asked.

"Mr. Yamashita almost told my classmates that I'm from North Korea. He almost messed everything up."

"Would it be such a big deal if he did?" asked Mrs. Lee, looking puzzled.

"You'll have to tell your friends sooner or later."

"People would be shocked. They'd stop being my friend and I'd be an outcast. People don't know how to act with things related to North Korea. I'm just a human but I can't escape it," replied Hana, looking more dejected than ever.

"Oh my dear child. You know, it's not your fault that people in North Korea are struggling. Maybe, when you're ready, you'll be able to tell the truth and I think you'll be pleasantly surprised at how ready people are to listen."

Still smiling cheerfully at Hana, Mrs. Lee patted her gently on the back before slowly plodding back into the kitchen.

"Maybe she's right," Hana said to herself.

"Maybe."

Keyword: community, identity, adaptation, coming out.

Discussion Questions

☐ Why do you think Hana is scared of her past coming out?
☐ Do you think that Mr. Yamashita has a responsibility to keep Hana's secret? Why/why not?

Activities

There are many kinds of 'identity'; a person might identify themselves as a supporter of a particular sports team, a user of a brand of computer and a voter of a particular political party all at once.

How might identity, how you think of yourself and how others think of you become complicated? Make a list of the ways you identify yourself and then a second list of how you think others think of you. Compare your two lists and consider the differences between the two.

Next, with a partner make a list about how you think of other and then see how similar their list and yours are.

Case study 9
Biting Off More than You Can Chew

Following the lunch break, Hana was feeling a little upset. While the students were eating, a minor dispute had occurred between her Japanese classmate, Takuya, and Aaron, from Canada. As is often the case with these things, it started over a misunderstanding.

Takuya had brought a can of fish as part of his lunch and on the label, attached to the side of the can, was written *King of Seafood!* Hana and Aaron, as yet unaccustomed to Japanese food, accepted Takuya's offer to share the contents of the can and, at first, enjoyed it very much.

"This is great, Takuya," Hana exclaimed.

"I've never had tuna like this before."

"Tuna?" replied Takuya.

"Oh no. This isn't tuna. This is whale."

Hana had no response to Takuya's comment, but she noticed Aaron's face slowly turning red.

"Whale? Are you serious? Takuya, how could you eat whale? It's full of mercury and really bad for us," Aaron spluttered.

"It's also totally immoral. Yuck! You're unbelievable."

"Wait a second, Aaron," interrupted Takuya.

"I think this is a cultural misunderstanding. I didn't know how strongly you felt about this. Don't forget, different people eat different things. Some Koreans eat dog and some French people eat snails. Some anti-whaling countries used to hunt whales for their oil. Don't be so narrow-minded," argued Takuya, now also clearly upset.

Choosing to remain silent, Hana shrank lower and lower into her chair. She had actually quite enjoyed the whale meat and had also eaten dog in the past. While she didn't think it sounded like a good idea to eat snails, she understood Takuya's point. At the same time, she realised that whales are rare, with many species on the verge of extinction.

With neither Aaron nor Takuya willing to compromise, things were

starting to get out of hand. Overhearing the disorder Mr. Yamashita, seated at the next table, interjected,

"Gentlemen, please. In my view you are both right and you are both wrong. Let's settle this with an intellectual debate. But let's make things interesting," Mr. Yamashita grinned mischievously.

"Aaron, you will lead the affirmative team, arguing that it's okay to eat animals like whale and dolphin. Takuya, you will be on the negative team, so it's your team's task to argue that these things are wrong. Okay? So, save the rest of this discussion for my class tomorrow and good luck!"

With that, Mr. Yamashita picked up his coffee and walked off in the direction of the staff room.

"Can something that tastes so good really be so bad?"

Hana pondered to herself on the way home from school. She was certain she would have to participate in the debate so as soon as she arrived home she started researching the anti-whaling issue and dolphin drive hunting.

Keyword food customs, tradition, morality, cultural difference.

Discussion Questions
- ☐ If you were Hana, which side of the debate would you want to join?
- ☐ How would you justify your point of view?
- ☐ What do you think about eating dog meat or snails?
- ☐ Do you think there is a line between pets and livestock? Why/why not?
- ☐ Are you for or against zoos/ aquariums/wildlife parks?

Activities

After watching the documentary, "The Cove," divide into two groups, A and B.

The role of Group A is to advocate and protect the traditional customs of the Taiji people in Japan.

The role of Group B is to argue that dolphin drive hunting is unnecessary and this outweighs its significance as a traditional practice.

Take some time to consider your key debate points and how you will present them. If possible, do some basic research on these issues to strengthen your argument.

Case study 10
Does *Hankuk-saram* Mean Korean?

Three months had already passed since the beginning of the semester. Hana's new school life in Osaka continued to be enjoyable, her international friends opening her eyes to many new things.

Another school day was drawing to an end. Hana was chatting to In-ho while she packed her bag to head home. During her time settling into life in the GCS Hana had become close friends with In-ho. As a *Zainichi* Korean, she felt a connection to him, remembering the things her parents had told her about her own *Zainichi* Korean background.

Just as they were preparing to leave, Junho and Chul, both representatives of the South Korean Student Association, wandered up to her. Hana felt a little uneasy. Although a good student, Junho was not very popular. His comments concerning the ethnic backgrounds of other students often seemed disrespectful. Someone had even told her that Junho had said *Zainichi* food is not authentic Korean cuisine. Furthermore, he had a tendency, Hana had noticed, to shun talking to non-Korean classmates and would speak mostly in Korean. Chul, on the other hand, seemed like a nice guy and got on well with everyone. It was a pity, Hana thought, that the two of them were as good as connected at the hip.

"Hana, can we talk to you for a moment?"

Junho asked, as Hana finished pushing the last of her textbooks into her bag.

"Is it just me or are you avoiding us in class? You don't even use Korean with us when we try to talk with you. And you've never once come to our Korean association activity group. Are you planning on coming some time or what?"

"Oh. I didn't mean to…I'm sorry," Hana stammered.

"I'll try to find time next week, if possible. But really, I'm kind of busy these days, so I'm not sure yet. Sorry if I don't make it," she trailed off, purposely avoiding eye contact with either boy.

"It's no problem, Hana," said Chul, encouragingly.

"We'd just love to have you come along and get to know everyone. I may be wrong, but is it because of your Korean accent, Hana?" Junho interrupted.

"We don't mind about your accent. It's obvious you are from somewhere in Gangwon-province, right? I could tell because my grandpa is also from Gangwon-province and I've got quite an ear for the dialect."

"It's no big deal," continued Junho.

"We just want to be your friends. We're all *Hankuk-saram* and we should stick together, right? Hey. I've got an idea. Let's go watch the South Korea-Japan soccer match and cheer on the Korean team."

Hana and In-ho glanced at each other, both feeling uncomfortable at what Junho had said.

"If you aren't going to come watch the soccer, then at least come and join our meeting next time," pushed Junho.

"We're preparing quite a few Korean events for the up-coming school festival."

"I'll see what I can do, guys. But no promises, okay?" Hana replied, glancing up at the clock. "I'll see you guys tomorrow. I've got a bus to catch."

Keyword: inclusion, exclusion, ethnic solidarity.

Discussion Questions

☐ Why do you think Hana has kept a distance from Junho and Chul?

☐ Have you ever had any similar experiences to Hana, separating yourself from people with whom you felt a strong difference of opinions? Explain what happened.

☐ Junho seems to be strongly patriotic towards South Korea and this makes Hana feel uncomfortable. Do you think it could be a problem to love your country? Discuss the pros and cons of patriotism.

Activities

In groups of 2-4 discuss and record your answers to the following:

"We/us" and "they/them" are terms that create categories and divide people. Think of some examples when these kinds of terms are used in everyday life.

What is the result of using this kind of language? Who does it benefit and who loses?

Case study 11
Hana Visits 'Nishi Nihon Detention Centre'

It was almost mid-morning, when a group of people alighted from a small commuter bus in a peaceful suburb just outside of Osaka. Hana was amongst them. Her application to the refugee-supporting NGO had been accepted and today was her first day of volunteering. Today's mission was to meet and talk to illegal migrants who had been caught by the police and whose status in Japan was under evaluation. Hana had also been asked to serve as an interpreter in her meeting with Ms. Cho, a Korean-Chinese lady who was fighting to stay in Japan.

"Welcome to Nishi Nihon Detention Centre," an employee greeted her.

"I hope the journey here was a pleasant one. And don't panic, your job today is simply to meet with two detainees and give them the chance to tell their story. It helps them to have visitors, especially people who are willing to listen."

Hana smiled nervously and followed the security staff through to the visitors' area.

"Gosh," she exclaimed. "It all looks so…normal."

"Well. It's not a five star hotel, but we try and make it liveable for detainees," replied the employee.

Having left her in the visitors' area momentarily, the employee returned with a man following close behind. Mr. Ali Welat had a robust, slightly weathered face and large hands that he would frequently wring together. He introduced himself to Hana and told her his story:

"I've been here for over two months. I'm from Turkey, but I'm Kurdish. I'm sure you already know too much about the tragedies of my people. I heard from a friend that Japan is a good country to live, so I bought a ticket to come here. First, I came here to earn money for my family. But while I was here I received word from a friend in Turkey that the government found out I was a member of radical student group supporting the independence of a Kurdish nation. Because I was scared I applied for asylum here in Japan. But the Japanese government doesn't seem to take care of people like me. I'm worried what might happen. What if they send me back to Turkey? I'm

scared the government will punish me," he explained, his voice trembling.

"The big problem, now that I'm here in Japan," he continued, "is that I don't know if I can prove I was a member of the student group. Nor do I know how to prove that I face persecution if I return to Turkey. Ironically, as I have applied for asylum here, the Turkish government will find out about my deportation if that happens. There is no way out. If I can stay here in Japan, I'll work in construction and live quietly. I don't want to cause anyone any problems. I'm not sure what's going to happen, but I want to stay in this country."

© Chung In-kyung

After the interview with Mr. Ali, Hana had another meeting with Ms. Hyang-jin Cho, a woman in her early forties. She shook Hana's hand and softly exclaimed that she was also very pleased she had come to visit.

Ms. Cho explained,

"I'm from Northeast China and I've lived in Japan for eight years. I was living here illegally and working in the kitchen of a local restaurant. The police arrested me earlier this year and brought me to the detention centre. I have a daughter. Actually, she's just a baby and her father is Japanese, but he's not my husband. I don't know if this means I can stay here in Japan or not. I'm appealing to the Ministry of Justice for special permission to stay here and be with my baby. I worry about her. She needs a mother."

Ms. Cho asked Hana to contact the father of her daughter and bring her back news. Hana said she would do her best.

Hana recognised that Mr. Ali and Ms. Cho both wanted to try and improve their lives. She felt sorry for them but was not sure if staying illegally in Japan was the right thing to do. As she made her way out of the detention centre she took a last look around.

Under her breath she mumbled,

"If everyone here has such a sad story, wouldn't it be better if Japan was more open to foreigners and refugees?"

Keyword

detention centre, illegal migration, persecution, asylum.

Discussion Questions

☐ Do you think Mr. Ali should be allowed to stay in Japan? Why/why not?

☐ Do you think Ms. Cho should be allowed to stay in Japan? Why/why not?

☐ If you met Mr. Ali or Ms. Cho, and you knew that they were living in Japan illegally, what would you say to them?

☐ How do you think civic groups help people like Mr. Ali and Ms. Cho?

☐ Japan continues to be reluctant to admit refugees into the country. Given that some individuals have been in Japan for years and have children and family in Japan how might humanitarian issues make their staying/deportation more difficult to rule on?

Activities

In groups of 2-4 write out the reasons why Mr. Ali and Ms. Cho should be allowed to stay in Japan. Then write out the reasons why they should not be allowed.

Use these points as the starting point for a discussion with your group.

Case study 12
Hana and Aaron Go to the Movies

Hana and Aaron were rounding off a busy week at school and needed to let off some steam. Aaron had asked Hana to go see a new South Korean film called *Crossing*. Aaron said it was a drama and he had wanted to see it for a while. To see if Hana was interested, he sent her a synopsis:

> *Crossing* tells the real story of the life of a North Korean coal miner who crosses illegally into China to get medicine for his wife. His wife passes away soon after he crosses the border and he is separated from his 11-year-old son who continues to search for him. *Crossing* stands for the experiences of many North Koreans during the famine of the mid-1990s, when an estimated one million people died. North Koreans looking for food or a better life couldn't go to South Korea directly because of the heavily guarded border. They had to cross into China and go through Southeast Asia to find safety. *Crossing* is not a film from the past, because the Chinese government still does not recognise North Koreans leaving their country as refugees and repatriates them back to North Korea.

Hana was surprised that such a film had been made and could not miss the chance to see it. She agreed to meet Aaron at 7pm, outside the movie theatre.

After getting their popcorn and soda, Hana and Aaron went inside and got settled in their seats. The lights went down and the film started rolling. Aaron had warned Hana that it was a tearjerker, but Hana had not prepared herself for this kind of film. She sat spellbound in her chair as the story of a family of North Korea refugees played out in front of her.

When the lights came up the audience started shuffling out of the theatre, Hana could not stand up. Aaron had not noticed how quiet she had been during the film but now, in the light, he could see she was still fixated on the screen. Unsure of what to say he placed his hand on her shoulder. "So? What did you think?" he asked.

Hana suddenly turned to Aaron and smiled, "It was fascinating and who'd have thought they'd make a film about North Korean refugees? I'm speechless. It was so realistic. So many North Koreans don't make it to start their lives in a new country."

"Wow. Okay. I'm glad you enjoyed it so much. How do you know so much about North Korean refugees? You sound like a TV presenter," Aaron quipped.

"I'm interested in this stuff, Aaron. I read an article that most North Korean refugees arrive in South Korea, but some of them fail to settle there and try to move to third countries such as the UK," Hana explained to Aaron.

"So far away from home," Aaron said.

"So far," replied Hana, wondering if Aaron knew her secret.

refugee, the stateless, defector, media.

☐ Discuss what you have heard about North Korean refugees. Why do you think they exist?

☐ What do you think the main challenges they face are?

☐ Imagine you are a refugee and you can't go back to your country. How do you live? What do you do to survive?

☐ What do you think society can do to help refugees and asylum seekers?

In groups of 2-4 discuss and record what you already understand about refugees in your country and in foreign countries.

Looking at popular culture and the media, what attitudes do you think are common towards refugees? What kind of stories (conflict, disaster, political disputes) are refugees usually associated with? What effect do you think this has on how people generally think about a refugee?

Case study 13
Hana Writes a Letter Home

Hana had been feeling homesick for quite some time. Her recent movie date with Aaron had made her feel further away from home and more concerned about her family. With the help of a refugee NGO she had learned of a way to send a letter and a small package to her family back home.

The NGO employee had advised her, "If you are going to write a letter to your family in North Korea, you have to make sure you hide your identity well. Otherwise, your family may be in danger. Just give your family little clues so they know it's you writing." With this in mind, early one Tuesday morning she shuffled sleepily across her bed and over to her desk. Hana picked up her pen and paused, what if the authorities recognised who she is? She would have to disguise her identity to keep her parents safe. She picked up her pen and began writing:

> Dear Dong-hyun and Suk-ja.
>
> I hope this letter finds you both happy and healthy. Suk-ja, I'm your cousin, Kyung-ok. Do you remember me? I was born in the middle of August. I used to love strawberry ice cream and I have a birthmark on my left ankle that you might remember.
>
> It seems like a lifetime ago that you and I used to play together in Osaka. Well, it has been over fifty years. I'm doing well here in Japan. I'm working hard to make enough money to have the life that we always wanted for each other.
>
> How are you? I miss you both a lot and sometimes regret my decision not to follow you to the fatherland. I'm sure that you are well taken care of in North Korea and I hope I can come and visit you soon.
>
> Suk-ja, do you still enjoy the steamed bread we used to eat as children? I wish I could have some now. How is your back? I

have included some medicine in this package, I hope it gets to you safely. I have also included some money. I hope you can use the money to buy some warm clothes for the winter.

    Suk-ja, I miss you very much and my care for you and Dong-hyun never wavers. If you can, please send me a family photo for the Lunar New Year celebration, that's the time when I miss you the most.

    I love you,
    Kyung-ok Lee.

The next day, just after the bell went, Hana quietly left school and took the bus to a post office on the other side of town where she bought several stamps. After sending her letter, she inquired about how to send a parcel. The postman seemed surprised at her request, "North Korea?" he had asked her, not sure if he had heard right. It was not good news, however. He gently informed her that government prevented items being sent to North Korea. Hana realised that the political tensions had affected the mailing system. She thought about her letter and was immediately worried it would not arrive safely. She could not stop thinking about it for the rest of the day.

Keyword: divided families, migration, communication channels.

Discussion Questions

- ☐ Do you think Hana made the right decision in leaving her family and home?
- ☐ Why do you think she cannot meet her family?
- ☐ Why is Hana advised not to say her real name when she writes to her family?
- ☐ Why do you think Hana misses her family the most during Lunar New Year?
- ☐ Try to imagine that you are a refugee, away from your family and friends and not knowing when you might meet them again. What do you miss the most about home? What do you tell your family in your letter?

Activities

In pairs, students write down reasons why they think people migrate. Once they have done this divide the list of reasons into:
  1) Situations when people move voluntarily
  2) Situations when people move involuntarily

Use the two lists to discuss the differences in reasons why people move and what makes one person a migrant and another a refugee.

Further, think about how people who migrate continue to maintain contact to the people they leave behind.

What kind of connections do migrants create and maintain?

Case study 13   Hana Writes a Letter Home

Case study 14
Is Reunification Necessary?

It was Wednesday at the GCS. Hana walked into the seminar room, greeting her friends with whom she had booked the room. Around the table the sound of students satisfying their hunger gradually gave way to the rustling of paper as each person prepared for the lunchtime discussion. Wednesday lunch was the time when Hana and some of her more enthusiastic friends would meet to discuss issues of culture, social affairs, and politics. Today's topic, raised by In-ho, was the reunification of the Korean peninsula.

Dusting off crumbs from several recently devoured biscuits, In-ho opened the discussion, asserting the importance of the reunification of the two Koreas. Using prepared notes he underlined his belief that *Zainichi* Koreans in Japan would benefit if the Korean peninsula were reunified in a peaceful way.

Junho did not agree with In-ho's thoughts,

"To South Koreans," he argued, "reunification is nothing but an economic burden since South Koreans will have to look after North Koreans and the younger generation like us will suffer the economic consequences. In-ho, you're being naïve and idealistic if you think that reunification can happen in anything but a chaotic way."

Chul hesitated before countering, "I don't agree with you, Junho. Some people may think that after 70 years, the division of the Korean peninsula will continue as the status quo. It's no easy thing for South Koreans to live with that. But if we consider how short seventy years of division is in the context of thousands of years of continuity, it's really just a blip. Reunification will happen sometime and I'm certain it will be welcomed by Koreans and their neighbours."

Attempting a more neutral approach to what he realised was already an impassioned debate, Aaron asked, "What about the international community, is there anything they could do to resolve the human rights and poverty issue in North Korea, prior to reunification?"

Junho again chimed in,

"There are only 30,000 North Koreans in South Korea right now and it's

already so hard for the state to support these individuals. Imagine if we have to try and support 25 million North Koreans – it's impossible!"

"If reunification is achieved, a unified Korea will have over 70 million people. It could have a huge economic reach. Thus, I believe that reunification is more of an opportunity than a risk," asserted Chul.

"Maybe South Koreans aren't yet ready to for reunification," Aaron pondered.

Takuya, Hana's Japanese classmate, made the most of the sudden lull in the debate, "I think, from Japan's side of things, reunification is a bad idea. Just think of how unstable a unified Korea would be and, if things did eventually work out, it would always be anti-Japanese. No, it's not something we'd want to see," he concluded.

"What about all the divided families?"

Hana suddenly blurted out.

"What about bringing together people who have been separated for so long? Isn't that more important than money?"

"Maybe you're right, Hana," Aaron replied.

"It sounds to me like this is more complicated than it looks. There's an economic perspective and then a humanitarian one. Actually, there's probably far more to consider than that."

Hana and In-ho glanced at each other, both shaking their heads in dismay. It seemed their classmates were not to be won over on the issue of reunification from the humanitarian perspective of families divided between the two Koreas. Just then the bell rang out, signalling the end of lunch.

"Okay everyone, great discussion today. Same time next week?"

Hana did not reply, packing up her lunch box in silence.

Keyword

division, unification, the cost of reunification, humanitarian.

Discussion Questions

☐ Do you think the reunification of the two Koreas is possible? Why/why not?

☐ Are you for or against the reunification of two Koreas? Justify your opinion.

☐ What do you consider members of the international community think about the reunification of the two Koreas? Explain your point of view.

Activities

Debate: Reunification: the pros and cons

Divide into two teams, with one side taking the affirmative, arguing for the reunification of the two Koreas and the other side arguing against it. Draw on the various ideas discussed above (humanitarian issues, economic issues, the right of a people to self-determination), as well as any further information you can find.

Case study 15
The New Girl: What is She?

JAPANESE KOREAN

Hana's class was abuzz with the news that a new girl was starting today. Mr. Yamashita had made the announcement that she would be joining halfway through the first period. Sure enough, just after 9am, there was a knock on the classroom door. In walked the principal, Mr. Kimura, dressed in his trademark grey, pinstriped suit which had earned him the nickname, "Al Capone," among the students. He was closely followed by a nervous looking girl in jeans, a white T-shirt and a red baseball cap. The principal whispered something to Mr. Yamashita before disappearing back out into the hallway, leaving the new girl standing awkwardly in front of the class.

"Ladies and gentlemen, this is Mariko," announced Mr. Yamashita, in his usual stern tone.

The new girl cleared her throat, "Actually, I prefer to be called Tina," she corrected him.

"It's my American name."

"Well Tina it is then," replied the unperturbed Mr. Yamashita.

"Now go and take a seat over there, beside Hana. She'll help you settle in."

Sliding her bag off her shoulder, Tina nudged her way between the desks until she got to the empty space next to Hana.

"Hi Tina, I'm Hana. I'm also quite new here, but I can show you how things work if you join us for lunch," offered Hana.

"That sounds perfect. Thanks, Hana," replied Tina.

Hana and Tina found seats with other students.

"Hey Tina, where are you from? You have kind of an American accent, right? And your cap tells me you love baseball," quizzed Takuya.

"What are you? You're pure Japanese, right?" he added.

"Pure Japanese? What does that even mean?" Tina, her face suddenly turning dark, replied.

"I hear this all the time and I'll tell you clearly now. My Dad is Japanese American. My mum is Korean American and I've lived most of my life in the U.S. I know what you're thinking; I'm *Hafu*, mixed. Right?"

"We're just curious about you, Tina. I guess you like Western food, yeah? I mean, you're American so I can show you a good pizza place near school," proposed In-ho, reassuringly.

"As you know, Japan has a long history and strong culture. We all should be proud of it. Tina, you're half Japanese and you should respect it, too," Takuya suddenly exclaimed.

The table became silent and Tina's face went bright red.

"That's the kind of attitude I have to deal with every time I move to a new school. You

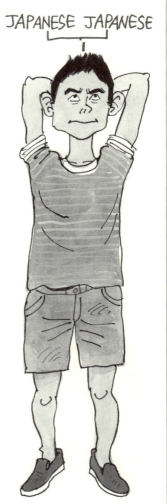
© Chung In-kyung

think just because both your parents are Japanese and you were brought up in Japan that you're 'pure'. Do you actually believe that makes you better than me? I'm proud to be Asian American, Japanese and Korean. It's the best of everything that makes me who I am and I feel sorry for people who feel threatened by that. Don't stereotype me."

"Sorry Tina," mumbled Takuya.

"I just think it's strange," he continued.

"My parents always tell me that I should feel proud to be Japanese. I just wanted to say the same thing to you, Tina."

"I always consider myself lucky to have a diverse background. I can speak three languages and, because of my father's work, I get to see the world," Tina replied.

"Takuya is a boy who respects Japanese tradition," interjected Hana.

"But, he has a lot to learn about respecting difference. Actually, many of us here have mixed backgrounds so you're in good company."

"Sorry everybody. I don't mean to be so sensitive. I just get this kind of thing everywhere I go in Japan and Korea. I sometimes feel like more of a thing on display than a human being. Takuya. No hard feelings, Okay?" Tina smiled.

"I guess we just need to get to know each other a bit more."

Takuya replied, his cheeks starting to blush.

Keyword *Hafu* or *Daburu*, mixed ethnicity, assimilation, stereotyping.

Discussion Questions
☐ What is the problem with seeing a people as 'pure'?
☐ Why can terms like 'mixed' and '*Hafu*' be hurtful to people?
☐ Why might Tina's new classmates want to know 'what she is'?

Case study 16
Hana's Big Secret

Mr. Yamashita stared out from behind his desk, hesitating momentarily to focus his eyes on the students before calling out, "Hana, I believe it's your turn to present your project. Would you please make your way up here?"

Clutching her notes in her hand Hana shuffled up to the front of the class and inserted her USB into the computer. Her hand was shaking as she slid the mouse pointer across the screen and paused over the file marked 'My Hometown'. Looking up, she gazed out at the faces of her friends.

"Everybody," she croaked, in a voice approaching a whisper, "My plan was to speak to you about *Zainichi* Koreans, but last night I had a realisation. The fact is that although we're all from different places, with different backgrounds, we're friends and our difference is what brings us together. I've been keeping a secret from you all and today I want to tell it to you."

Aaron and Yumi glanced inquiringly at each other. What could it be that Hana had been keeping a secret? And why?

Hana again moved the blinking arrow over the file, this time double clicking without hesitation. The TV lit up and the words, 'My Hometown: Sinuiju, North Korea,' filled the screen. Below the title was a picture of Hana surrounded by several smiling people.

"I'm from Sinuiju, North Korea. This is my family. They're still there," she explained.

The class was silent. Gripped by nerves, Hana suddenly lost her voice entirely. Mr. Yamashita stood up from his chair. "Fascinating, Hana. Please continue. I'm sure you have a lot to tell us."

"Go on," called out Aaron.

"Don't stop now, Hana."

Hana took a deep breath and scrolled to the next screen.

"I was born in Sinuiju, it's a town on the border with China. It's famous for the beautiful mountains you can see in this picture and the ponds that freeze over in the winter where I used to go ice-skating with my friends. In summer my family and I used to roast corn beside the river next to my home and in the winter we'd heat up the *ondol* with coal bricks from the market. I know that maybe you all think that North Korea is a terrible place, but my family's life there was good until the early 1990s."

Hana clicked on the mouse and the next slide popped up on the TV. It was a picture of people on a dock, waving flags and cheering, while others were calling out to them from a large ship.

"My family returned to North Korea from Japan in 1961 as a part of the repatriation of *Zainichi* Koreans. My parents were just children then and they thought that North Korea would give them the things they couldn't have in Japan because of the prejudice they faced from being Korean. When they arrived in North Korea, however, life was very hard. But they lived near many others from Japan and people helped each other in times when there wasn't enough food to eat or coal to burn."

The screen changed again and the class let out a collective gasp.

"My family had a really hard time in the late 1990s and for the early years of the 2000s. This was a time called the 'Arduous March'. Often there wasn't enough food for ordinary people in North Korea," explained Hana, pointing to the picture of a thin, hungry looking child on the TV screen.

"It was around this time that many North Koreans suffered from a food shortage and malnutrition. So many people died and my family decided I needed to leave my hometown. I didn't want to leave my family and friends behind. I didn't want to leave the mountains and rivers, but I knew I might not survive if I stayed in North Korea. My family didn't have enough food to support me and we thought I could find work and food in China."

Hana's voice was starting to waver but she noticed that her classmates were engrossed by what they were hearing so she continued, clicking to a map of China. Pointing to the map, she explained, "I left my home and illegally crossed the border into China, where I worked for a while.

But I soon realised that it wasn't safe for me and if the Chinese police caught me they would send me back to North Korea, where I could get in big trouble. Because my family came to North Korea during the repatriation project, I knew I had the chance of coming to Japan. So when things didn't work out in China, that's what I decided to do. With the help of some refugee NGO workers here in Japan, I contacted people from the Japanese embassy and, after a while, I came to Osaka."

Hana now turned back to the class.

"I wanted to tell you all this because it's hard hiding myself. I miss my family, my friends, and my hometown. I'm happy to be here in Japan but without my mother and father here it's sometimes very tough for me. Thank you for listening, I hope you all understand."

Aaron and Yumi broke the silence, taking the lead as the class burst into applause.

"Hana, that was great," encouraged Yumi.

"Of course we understand. Your hometown looks very beautiful and you must miss your family terribly. From now on, you don't have to hide anything, we're your friends, no matter where you are from."

The class began to settle down and Mr. Yamashita again rose from behind his desk, facing the class.

"Today we learnt about Hana's hometown. We learnt about her family and the hardships they have endured. Most importantly, for all of you, we learnt about what it means to be a global citizen, to understand that all people, whether they are from North Korea or Japan, Canada or South Korea, need family and friends around them. Especially when you are away from your family and hometown, like Hana, it's your friends that provide a starting point for you to grow in your new environment. Hana."

He said, still facing the class.

"We're proud of you. What you did today was a brave thing indeed and

I'm honoured to be your homeroom teacher."

This time it was Hana's cheeks that blushed bright red.

"Hey Hana, feeling a bit bashful?" Takuya teased.

Keyword: famine, displacement, denial and acceptance.

Discussion Questions

☐ Why do you think Hana kept her origin a secret from her classmates?
☐ Why do you think Hana felt the need to reveal her secret?
☐ Why is there a stigma attached to refugees?
☐ What do you know about North Korea and North Korean refugees? Do you think your knowledge is accurate?

Activities

In groups of 2-4 discuss and record your answers to the following:

How do you think you would react to hearing Hana's secret?

Why do you think you would feel this way?

Epilogue

This textbook was developed out of the research and collective passion of researchers from Australia, Japan, New Zealand and South Korea. It focuses on key themes of migration, identity, and mutual understanding between people of diverse backgrounds.

The authors would like to think that Hana continued to thrive in the Global Citizens' School and went on to study at university. She would have undoubtedly faced further hurdles as she continued with the challenging process of settling into life in Japan but, with support from those around her, she would certainly have overcome them. There are many people like Hana in our world. We may not always get to meet them and, if we do, we may not even recognise that they are such a person.

Perhaps the most important thing to take from this text and the story of Hana is that we should always strive to be reflective regarding our attitudes towards others, towards ideas and people who might make us feel uncomfortable and also towards the images and stories we see in the media. If this textbook encourages the reader to question a fact or an idea that they have previously taken for granted, then it can be considered as a small success on the road to a better, peaceful society.

This text was written by three different authors: Dr. Kyungmook Kim, Professor of Peace Studies at Chukyo University, Markus Bell, Ph.D. candidate at the Australian National University, and Susan Menadue-Chun, Ph.D. candidate at Rikkyo University. The authors would further like to thank the following people for their contributions: Jiro Ishimaru, Hana Lee, Chung In-kyung, Christine Bell, Sandra Fahy, Sam Macdonald, Jeremy Thomas, Eun-jeong Song, Katsuyuki Aoyagi, Mariko Hayashi, and Melisanda Berkowitz.

Markus Bell
The Australian National University

● About the Authors and the Illustrator

Kyungmook Kim
Kyungmook Kim is Professor of Peace Studies at Chukyo University, Japan. His recent academic concern is on the re-migration of North Korean diaspora. He graduated from Hankuk University of Foreign Studies, Seoul (B.A.) and received his M.A. and Ph.D. from the University of Tokyo.

Markus Bell
Markus Bell is a doctoral candidate in the anthropology department of the College of Asia and the Pacific, in the Australian National University. He works on matters of migration, refugees, identity, and memory and has published widely on these issues.
He can be contacted at <mpsbell@gmail.com>.

Susan Menadue-Chun
Susan Menadue-Chun is a Ph.D. candidate at Rikkyo University, Tokyo. Her current research focuses on the changing identities of the Chongryon school teachers and community. She is also a research fellow at the Ryukoku University's Ahn Jung Geun Peace Centre.

Chung In-kyung
Cartoonist. She is Assistant Professor of Manga Studies at Tokyo Polytechnic University. She received her Ph.D. from Kyoto Seika University in 2006.
Her work can be found from <http://chunginkyung.com>.

プロローグ

　本教材は2012年11月から2014年10月までの2年間に行われたトヨタ財団研究助成プログラムの研究成果（研究課題番号 D12-R-0657「海外へ再移住する『脱北者』たちの理想と現実 —— トランスナショナル・ネットワークの活用とボーダー・コントロールの視点から」）の一部であります。

　これは、主に韓国に定住していた脱北者たちが韓国を離れ、ヨーロッパ、北米、オーストラリア、日本等の第三国に再移住を試みる過程を扱った研究であり、日本とオーストラリアに拠点を置く研究者たちによる新しいチャレンジでもありました。

　何よりも脱北者たちが今まで定住先として選んできた韓国から離れていく現象をどのように捉えるべきなのか、という問題の設定が新しい課題でありました。確かに、韓国政府の脱北者に対する政策はさまざまな試行錯誤を繰り返してきましたが、諸外国の難民支援政策よりも手厚い支援であることには異論がありません。にもかかわらず、脱北者たちが韓国を離れて欧米諸国などに再移住するという事実からわかることは、韓国の支援制度にもいくつもの改善点があるということです。韓国における受入れ体制の課題、第三国に再移住しようとする動機、そして再移住先で脱北者が経験する状況という観点から制度の改善が摸索されるべきでしょう。なぜならば、脱北者たちが経験した心理的、社会的、文化的な葛藤は南北コリアの分断を超えて、北東アジアに暮らす人びとにまで多大なる影響を及ぼすからです。

　これらの課題を克服するにはさまざまな方法があり得ますが、現行の教育制度の活用、そして教材作りという方法を通じて、人びとが思いもしなかった問題点を改めて見直し、理解することが大切なのではないかと考え、教材開発を進めることになりました。執筆者たちは、この教材の活用が複雑かつ、時には感情的になりがちの問題の解決への最初の一歩になることを願っています。

　もちろん、この教材を活用する方法に正解は存在しませんし、教材を通じて得られる発見も多種多様でしょう。それが本教材を活用する上での特徴であり期待される効果でもあります。多様性のなかから得られる意見の違いを発見し、また異なる見解をどのように尊重するかという悩みのなかから文化の違いと共存の大切さが深まることを期待しております。本書にある会話、考え方、異なる意見が、融和や共存の大切さを理解し、文化の違いを考慮するための道具箱になることを願っています。関連して、本書で使用されている英語の表記は「グローバル英語（Global English / World

Englishes)」という新しい概念の普及に基づき、英国式、米国式に限定せず、原則、混在を許す形としています。

　脱北者に対する漠然とした同情は問題解決には役立ちませんし、むしろそれが人を傷つけてしまうことすらあります。私たちは日常生活で誰かについて知りたいことがあるときに、失礼になるかと思い聞くことができない場合があります。北朝鮮から来た人びとに対して何かを知りたいとき、どのように聞くべきなのか、それとも聞くべきではないのかという戸惑いが頻繁に生じます。本教材は、それらの悩みをすべて解決してくれることはできませんが、その問題についての関心をもたらすきっかけを作ることができると考えます。

　より多くの人びとが文化の違いを理解し、多様性を許容する社会づくりを求めるのであれば、私たちの生活空間は今まで以上に平和で豊かになるでしょう。本教材の活用を通じてそのようなきっかけづくりがなされることを願います。最後に教材を開発する上で支援を惜しまなかった多くの方々に感謝の気持ちを伝えさせていただきます。本書には中京大学の「2015年度特定研究助成共同研究B（代表 ── 風間 孝教授）」の一部予算が使用されているということは特記しておきます。この場を借りて、中京大学ならびに共同研究のメンバーに御礼申し上げます。

中京大学　国際教養学部教授　金 敬黙（キム ギョンムク）

「地球市民学校」(The Global Citizens' School)

　この教材の舞台になっている「地球市民学校」(Global Citizens' School: GCS) は、2007年に日本と韓国に暮らす教育関係者、研究者、ビジネス界の人びとの熱い思いによって建てられたという設定の架空の学校です。「地球市民学校」の創設に貢献した個々人は、学生たちが「越境」というキーワードを合言葉に、世界で活躍する市民になることを夢見ています。この学校が日本にあることや一人ひとりの国籍などは、特別な意味を持ちません。

　長年の間、日本では、コリア系の学校は北朝鮮系と韓国系に分類されてきました。日本の学校は、日本人のための教育機関としての役割を果たすことを当然としてきました。「地球市民学校」は、日本と朝鮮半島の歴史的な葛藤や問題を乗り越え得る教育機関として期待されて誕生した学校です。この学校の歴史教育は、日本の、朝鮮半島の、そして国際的な視野から取り組まれています。これは、差異を乗り越え、日本人、韓国人、朝鮮人、または在日コリアンとしてだけではなく、地球市民として自分の居場所を模索することに役立つという理念に基づくものです。

　主人公ハナが通うこの学校は大阪の郊外にあるという設定です。地域社会からの寄付、そして日本人、在日コリアンのビジネス界の人びとの支援によって支えられています。小さな学校ですが、教師や学生たちは世界各地から集まっており、国や民族の違いを乗り越える理念を共有しています。

　「地球市民学校」は発展途上の学校です。いまだ北東アジア地域には和解と平和を妨げる政治問題や歴史課題が山積しています。だからこそ日本や朝鮮半島の政治に揺さぶられず独立性を保とうと試みています。草の根、越境性の精神のもと、人びとの平和的な共存を模索することを心がけています。

目次

プロローグ　中京大学 国際教養学部教授　金 敬黙(キムギョンムク)　3

「地球市民学校」(The Global Citizens' School)　5

登場人物の紹介（キャラクター・プロフィール）　8

ケーススタディ 1　「地球市民学校」での新生活　10

ケーススタディ 2　ハナがブログを始める　12

ケーススタディ 3　由美の秘密　14

ケーススタディ 4　国家代表になるための条件　18

ケーススタディ 5　歴史は苦手　22

ケーススタディ 6　ハナが民族（朝鮮）学校に行く　24

ケーススタディ 7　ヘイトクライム　27

ケーススタディ 8　山下先生が秘密を漏らしそうになってしまった　30

ケーススタディ 9　伝統文化それとも殺戮？　34

ケーススタディ 10　韓国人とコリアンは同じ事なの？　37

ケーススタディ 11　ハナが西日本入国管理局に行く　41

ケーススタディ 12　ハナとアーロンの映画鑑賞　45

ケーススタディ 13　ハナの手紙　47

ケーススタディ 14　南北コリアの統一は必要？　51

ケーススタディ 15　転校生、彼女は何者？　54

ケーススタディ 16　ハナの秘密　57

エピローグ　オーストラリア国立大学 博士課程　マーカス・ベル　62

登場人物の紹介 (キャラクター・プロフィール) © Chung In-kyung

ハナ Hana

ハナのバックグランドは複雑であり、本人もこのことを気にしています。ハナは北朝鮮で生まれ育ちました。彼女の両親と祖父母は1959年から1984年の間に行われた「帰国事業」で日本から北朝鮮に渡った元在日朝鮮人たちでした。彼女が15歳の時、彼女の将来を案じた両親は、より明るい未来をハナに与えるために中国に逃亡させることにしました。不法越境者として隠れ住むことになった中国での生活環境は予想以上に厳しかったのですが、ハナや家族にとっても危険が伴うため、北朝鮮に戻ることもできない状況でした。幸い、日本の難民支援NGOの手助けによって17歳の誕生日が過ぎた直後、日本に来ることができました。脱北者支援を行うNGOのサポートによってハナが元在日朝鮮人の家族であることが証明できたからです。その後、アルバイトをしながら夜間学校に通い、日本語や英語、そして中国滞在中に遅れが生じてしまった勉強に追いつくため頑張ってきました。

夜間学校で一生懸命学んだハナは、NGOのサポートを得て、大阪郊外にある「地球市民学校」に通えることになりました。「地球市民学校」は「国境なき若者」を育成する夢を掲げたインターナショナル・スクールに近い学校です。したがって、ハナのクラスメイトたちは世界各地から集まってきています。現在19歳のハナは、他のクラスメイトよりも年上なのですがそのことは内緒にしています。ただ、ハナにとっての秘密はこればかりではありません。クラスメイトに知られないように北朝鮮から来たことはすべて秘密にしているのです。そのため、ハナは韓国出身ということになっています。彼女の秘密はみんなにばれないで済むのでしょうか。

由美 Yumi

由美はコリア系の日本人です。由美はアイデンティティ問題で悩んでいて、そのため彼女は周囲に自分の出自を伏せています。以前通っていた日本の学校でそのことがばれるのではないかと悩み続け、それを心配した由美の両親は、由美が日本人やコリアンにこだわらず地球市民として育ってほしいという願いから「地球市民学校」に転校させることを決めました。

ヒャンミ Hyang-mi

ヒャンミは朝鮮学校に通うハナの友人です。ヒャンミは自らのエスニック・アイデンティティをオープンにしつつ、「祖国」としての北朝鮮とのつながりを感じています。したがって、在日コリアンであることを周囲に話していますし、在日コリアン・コミュニティと緊密な関係を保っています。けれども学校の外では日本語をしゃべり、最新の日本のファッションに憧れている、他の日本人の若者と何ひとつ変わらない女子高生です。

インホ In-ho

インホは在日コリアン3世です。彼はサッカーが大好きで、特に在日コリアンのサッカー選手である鄭大世(チョンテセ)選手の大ファンでもあります。

アーロン　Aaron

アーロンはハナのクラスメイトで、ハナにとっての初めてできた欧米出身の友だちです。彼もハナに負けないほど複雑な出自背景を持っています。アーロンは、カトリック教徒とプロテスタント教徒間の宗教紛争が長引いた北アイルランドで、カトリックの家庭に生まれました。宗教対立が続く時期に、アーロン一家はカナダに移住し、今は英国とカナダの国籍を持っています。アーロンは交換留学生として「地球市民学校」に通い、一生懸命日本語を勉強しながら、多様な文化的背景を持つクラスメイトについていろいろと学び始めています。

卓也　Takuya

卓也もハナのクラスメイトです。大阪生まれで日本の小学校と中学校を卒業しました。「地球市民学校」には高校から入学しました。それは卓也を地球市民に育てたいという卓也の両親の願いによるものでした。陽気でいたずら好きの少年であるために、時にはクラスメイトとトラブルを起こしてしまうこともあります。

山下先生　Mr. Yamashita

山下先生は歴史教科を担当するハナの担任教師です。日本人の山下先生は2007年の「地球市民学校」設立以来、この学校で教えてきました。学校でハナの秘密を知る限られた人の一人ですが、だからといってハナを特別扱いするわけではありません。厳格な性格の持ち主ですが、山下先生の心はとても暖かく彼の生徒たちが地球市民になれるように情熱を注いでくれます。

マリコ（ティナ）　Mariko/Tina

マリコ（ティナ）は「地球市民学校」への転校生です。転校生であるにもかかわらず、彼女の個性的かつ自信に満ちた行動が注目を集めます。マリコ（ティナ）のお父さんは日系アメリカ人（ジャパニーズ・アメリカン）で、お母さんはコリアン・アメリカンです。お父さんの仕事の関係上、彼女は世界各地で生活した経験を持ちます。マリコという日本名を持ちながらもティナという英語名をより好んでいます。

ジュンホとチョル　Junho and Chul

ジュンホとチョルの二人は「地球市民学校」で学ぶ韓国出身の留学生です。二人とも韓国人留学生会 (the South Korean Students' Association at the GCS) の活動に積極的に参加しています。この会では二週間ごとに会合が開かれ、朝鮮半島の文化と歴史について議論されます。

ケーススタディ１
「地球市民学校」での新生活

　これから転校する新しい学校の前で、ハナは駅から乗ってきたバスを降りた。サッカー場につながる学校の正門に「地球市民学校」という表札を見つけ、大きな声で読み上げてみたハナは、「これっていったいどういう意味なのかしら？」と首を傾げた。
　白い校舎から眼鏡をかけた背の高い男性が彼女の方に向かって歩いてくる姿を見つけたため、ハナにはそれ以上そのことについて深く考える余裕がなかった。
「ハナ？　リ・ハナだよね？」
　彼は握手の手を差し伸べる前に確認した。
「ようこそ、ハナ。僕は地球市民学校で君の担任を務める教員の山下だよ」
　彼はハナが応える間も与えず「僕について来て」と続けた。
　ハナは山下先生との距離が離れすぎないように小走りでついていき、建物に入り階段を上った。廊下の壁には様々な現場体験学習のポスターが飾られていた。「フィリピン・ボランティア活動」というものもあれば、「カンボジアでの学校建設のための資金集め」というものもあった。山下先生が廊下の角を曲がり教室に入っていったので、ハナも彼の後について教室に入っていった。
「ようこそ、ハナ。ここがこれからハナが学ぶ教室です。君の座席には名前が貼ってあるよ。北朝鮮からの学生を迎えることになってとても嬉しく思います」
　山下先生は眼鏡越しで温かく笑っていた。
「実を言いますと……」
　ハナは戸惑いつつお願いした。
「私が北朝鮮から来たことを他の人たちに話さないでください」
「ほう、本当にそれが良いと思うのかね？」
　山下先生は心配そうにそう聞いた。
「私はその方が良いと思います。私が韓国出身だとしておけば、皆さんも驚かないと思います。私は、皆さんが北朝鮮のことをどのように考えているか知っているので、ことをややこしくしたくないのです」とハナは説明した。
「そうですか。もしその方が、気が楽になるのであればそうしてあげますよ。しかしハナ、この学校は人の出身地なんかでアイデンティティを決めつけたりしないんですよ。ここでは、一人ひとりの個性が国籍とかエスニシティとかよりも大切にされています」

「よくわかりました、山下先生。ありがとうございます。でもまだちょっと気持ちの準備ができていないので……」

「あなたの秘密は内緒にしておきます、ハナ。あなたが一日も早く慣れて友だちを作れるように手伝ってあげましょう」

　山下先生は再度強調した。

「ところで歴史は好きですか？　僕は毎週テストをするのを楽しみにしているんですよ」

「参ったな〜。これから大変な一年になりそう」

　ハナは心の中でそう思った。

キーワード	**地球市民、国籍、エスニシティ、脱北者**
ディスカッション	□ なぜ、ハナは彼女の出身地について他のクラスメイトに秘密にすることを望んだのでしょうか。 □ 山下先生が言った、「一人ひとりの個性が国籍とかエスニシティとかよりも大切にされています」とはどのような意味でしょうか。
アクティビティ	２〜３人でグループをつくり、あなたはどれだけ多くのアイデンティティを持っていて、それらはどのように形成されているのか話し合いましょう。たとえば、家族、地域、ジェンダーをめぐるアイデンティティなどです。 　どのアイデンティティが最も重要で、またその理由はなぜですか。

ケーススタディ2
ハナがブログを始める

　今日も大阪は雨が降っていて、そのせいかハナはベッドからなかなか起きられない。目覚まし時計が激しく鳴るたびに、ハナは手を長く伸ばして、アラームのボタンを押しては再び布団の中にもぐりこんでいく。何度もこれを繰り返した挙句、ハナは仕方なく身を起こし、パソコンの前に座り、メールをチェックし始めた。

　新着メッセージが0件であると確認すると、ハナは「なら助かるわ」と呟いて、今度はソーシャル・ネットワーク・サービスの「Friendbook」をチェックし始めた。

　彼女の友人がアップした朝食の写真や書き込みをスクロールしながら、「面白くない内容ばかり……」と不満げに呟いた。近頃ハナは、自らの立場を他人に正直に語れないことに対するもどかしさと苛立ちを抱き、自分も知らないうちにモヤモヤとしていたのである。

　「もしも、私がブログを始めたら、きっとびっくりするような内容になるわ。日本に暮らす若い北朝鮮人女性の日常生活をつづるブログであると知ったら、みんな驚いてしまうはず」と思いつつも、ハナは同時に、そんなブログを自分が書いていることが学校の友だちにばれてしまったら、とんでもないことになるだろうという恐怖と不安も抱いていた。ハナはパソコン画面に反射する自分の顔を見つめながら決心した。

　「よし、私のストーリーをブログに書くことにしよう。でも私だと特定されないように、登場人物や場所、時間などについては細心の注意を払わないと」

　洗顔や歯磨きもせずパジャマ姿のままで、ハナは無料のブログサイトを検索し続けた。窓の外では冷たい雨が降り続いていた。新規入会することにしたブログに彼女の基本情報を入力した後、ブログ・デザインのレイアウトを選び、基本設定の情報を入力した。

　あとはもっとも重要な本文を書き込むだけだ。ハナは心臓の鼓動が少しずつ激しくなっているのを感じた。ブログの本文「作成」のボタンをクリックした。真っ白な新しいページが開いた。まるで次のコマンドを待ちきれないかのようにカーソルが落ち着きなく点滅していた。ハナは目をそっと閉じ、キーボードに指を添え、深呼吸をしてからブログを書き始めた。

　「私は北朝鮮から来ました。そう、脱北者であります。私の人生は普通の人とそれほど変わらないものでした。昼は学校で学び、友だちと遊ぶ普通の暮らしでした。しかし、ある日、そんな日常生活が突如一変し、私は友人や家族や国から離れなければな

らなくなりました」

キーワード　　**ソーシャルメディア、ライフストーリー、コミュニケーション**

ディスカッション

☐ ハナのように特別な事情がありながらも、そのことをどのように表現すればよいか分からない人にとって、新しいデジタル・メディアの長所は何でしょうか。

☐ ブログやツイッターなどのデジタル・メディアの問題点や弊害について話し合ってみましょう。

アクティビティ

　グループに分かれて、どのようにブログをデザインし、始めるか議論しましょう。

　スポーツや音楽、グルメなどテーマを決めてブログの運営方針やルール、役割の担当などについて話し合ってみましょう。誰が写真をアップするのか、誰が管理マネージャーになるのかなども話し合いましょう。これを今学期の共通課題として捉え、グループ内で運営してみましょう。

ケーススタディ 3
由美の秘密

　ハナが新しい学校生活を始めて間もないころ、担任の山下先生は、ハナが由美という日本人学生と親しくなって、彼女からいろいろな助けを得られるように配慮した。
「ハナ、学校生活は緊張するでしょ。もしよかったら、お互いがもっと親しくなれるように食事でも一緒にしない？」と由美がある日誘ってくれた。
　ハナは誘いに応じ、由美が案内する焼肉屋にいった。
「焼肉屋さんがリラックスするのにいいかな〜と思ってね」
　由美はお肉をトングでひっくり返しながら言った。
「とても美味しいわ、由美。こんなにおいしい焼肉は食べたことがないかもしれない」
「今日はハナちゃんの歓迎式よ、だから御馳走させてちょうだい」
「いやいや、そんなのダメよ」とハナは遠慮する。
「心配しないで、私はこのお店の経営者と知り合いなのよ」と由美は微笑む。
　それから数か月の間、二人は多くの時間を共に過ごした。そしてとても仲良しの友だちになった。AKB48や東方神起など、好きな芸能人についても話した。英語の上達のために二人で一緒に勉強した。また、女性雑誌「セブンティーン」の占いを読んで理想の男性像についての話でも盛り上がった。しかし二人の間に強い絆が生まれ始めているにもかかわらず、由美がなかなか彼女の家族や以前の学校生活について語ろうとしないことが、ハナには気になっていた。
　そんなある日、アーロンがハナにささやいた。
「ジュンホとチョルが昨夜、コリアン・レストランで食事をした時に、由美の両親がそこで働いているのを見かけたらしいんだ。以前、文化祭の時に学校に来た由美の両親と挨拶したことがあるから確かだそうだ。彼ら曰く、由美はコリアンに間違いないんだってさ」
「彼女がコリアンだったら、なぜ私にそのことを言ってくれないのかしら？」とハナは不思議に思った。
「由美のお父さんは、30店近くの焼肉チェーンを経営しているビジネスマンだよ」とさらにアーロンは続けた。
　ハナは由美と以前食事に出かけた時に、スタッフが二人にとりわけ親切であったことを思い出した。
「あのお店も由美の両親が経営している店だったのかしら？」

ハナは以前北朝鮮で祖母から聞いた、在日コリアンのことや帰国事業の背景について思い出した。
「私と由美ちゃんは同じ在日コリアンなのかもね」とハナは思った。
　でもハナは由美に直接そのことについて聞くことがためらわれた。もしかしたら由美が恥ずかしがり屋である理由は、由美の「ベールに包まれたアイデンティティ」と関係しているのかもしれない。ハナはモヤモヤした気持ちが高まり、山下先生に在日コリアンについてもっと詳しく訊いてみることにした。
「ハナ、先生が思うに、これをプロジェクト学習のテーマにして在日コリアンの歴史やハナの家族・親族について調べてみると良いと思います」と山下先生はアドバイスしてくれた。
「おそらくハナも知っている通り、在日コリアンの多くは日本による朝鮮半島の植民地化の結果、日本に渡ってくるようになりました」と説明してくれた。
「1945年の日本の敗戦によって、朝鮮半島は日本の支配を脱し、多くの朝鮮人がふるさとへ戻りましたが、60万人以上の人びとが日本に残りました。その後、旧植民地の人びとは外国人とされました。以前から強かった民族的な差別を避けようとして、多くの在日コリアンは引き続き通称名を使い続け、朝鮮半島出身者であることを隠すようになったのです」と山下先生は加えた。
　ハナは在日コリアンの歴史に興味を抱くとともに、在日コリアンが自らのアイデンティティを隠さなければならないという現実があることを悲しく思った。ハナは、先生のアドバイスを得て、在日コリアンのことをプロジェクト学習のテーマにすることにした。まずは在日コリアンともっと触れあおうと、ハナは地下鉄に乗って鶴橋のコリアタウンに行ってみることにした。鶴橋の町を歩きまわってハナの気分は少し落ちついた。多くの看板がハングルと日本語で書かれていた。商店の店員たちは日本語と韓国語でお客さんを相手にし、キムチや焼き肉を供する韓国・朝鮮料理の食堂もあった。
「これが在日コリアン社会の縮図なのね」
　彼女の好奇心がますます高まった。
　日本国籍に帰化をすることや、その後朝鮮半島出身者の子孫であることを隠し続けるのはやはり、民族的な差別問題が原因であろう、とハナは考えた。帰路につきなが

ら、ハナは自分の秘密について考え始めた。いつになれば友だちに本当の自分のことを言えるのだろうか、と。

キーワード

帰化、通称名で生きる、在日コリアンであることを隠す、アイデンティティ、エスニシティ、国籍

アクティビティ

　2～4人でグループをつくって、次の問いに関連する議論を行い、あなたの答えを記してください。

□ アイデンティティを隠すということはどのようなことでしょうか。

□ なぜ、由美はインターナショナル・スクールに通う今でも、彼女の出自を隠し通そうとするのでしょうか。

□ もしあなたがハナであるとしたら、由美に彼女の秘密を知っていることを伝えますか。

□ 由美と似たようなアイデンティティの葛藤を経験しそうなマイノリティ集団について話し合ってみましょう。

ケーススタディ 4
国家代表になるための条件

　FIFA ワールドカップが始まった。ハナが通う「地球市民学校」はサッカーの話題で大いに盛り上がっている。昼休みになるとハナのクラスメイトはスター選手に関する情報を交わし、またどのチームがベスト 16 に進出するかの予想で賑わっている。この日の昼休みも、インホ、ジュンホ、アーロンはセミナー・ルームに陣取って、彼らの憧れの選手について話していた。インホは鄭大世(チョンテセ)選手の大ファンである。
「僕は彼について知らないことなんてないよ。いつか彼のようになってみせる」
　興奮気味にインホは言った。
「ごめん、インホ。鄭大世っていったい誰？」
　アーロンが不可解な表情を浮かべながら聞いた。
「ビッグスターのことは一通り、押さえているんだけどなぁ」
「マジかよ？　鄭大世のことを知らないの？　よし、教えてあげよう。鄭大世は在日コリアン 3 世の選手さ。日本生まれで、韓国、そしてドイツのブンデスリーガでも活躍したんだ。彼が有名になった理由の一つには、2010 年の FIFA ワールドカップで北朝鮮代表として活躍したからさ」
　インホは目を輝かせながら彼のヒーローについて詳しくそして熱く語った。
「僕も在日コリアン 3 世じゃないか。だから彼は僕にとってのロール・モデルでもあるんだ。もし僕も頑張れば、韓国か日本の代表に選ばれるかもしれない。僕は別に北朝鮮代表になりたいとは思わないけれど、在日コリアンとして鄭大世の立場はよくわかるんだ」
　他方、韓国からの留学生であるジュンホはインホの発言に戸惑っていた。頭をかきながらジュンホはこう言った。
「悪いけど、僕に言わせれば、鄭大世はただの日和見主義にしか見えないんだ。彼が韓国籍を持っているのであれば、鄭大世は韓国の代表選手になる資格しか持っていないはず。彼がインホのヒーローであることはよくわかるけど、日本と韓国、そしてドイツで選手生活をして、韓国の代表選手になる努力もしないまま北朝鮮代表になるのは、個人的にはちょっといただけないと思うよ。僕のお父さんが言うんだ。国籍は運命のようなものだってね。穴の開いた靴下のように簡単に履き替えるものじゃないんだと。特にコリアンにとって、植民地支配の悲しい経験があるからこそ、自分の国に対する一層強い誇りを抱くべきなのだとね」

「ちょっと待てよ」

アーロンが割り込んだ。

「僕だって植民地化と分断の歴史の国から来ているんだぜ。多くの国がこの苦痛を経験して耐えてきたけれど、国籍なんかよりも、自分自身が母国をどう思うかがもっと大切なんじゃないかな。もし鄭大世が彼なりの役割をはたせるのであれば、北朝鮮の代表になっても別にかまわないんじゃないかな。もし彼が偉大なサッカー選手なのであれば、どの国のユニフォームを着ても輝くはずだよ。僕は北アイルランドであれカナダであれ、チャンスがあれば、どちらの国でも自分なりにそのチャンスを活かしたいと思う」

やがて彼らは試合の話題に戻り、少なくとも今は政治よりもサッカーそのものがもっと大切である、ということで落ち着いた。ハナは誰の立場に賛同できるのか、また何が国籍や民族を意味するのかよく理解できなかった。自分はいったいどこに属しているのだろうか。私は韓国人なのか、それとも北朝鮮人なのか。それとも私は在日コリアンなのだろうか。そんな疑問が次々と浮かんでくるのであった。

| キーワード | **エスニシティ（民族）、国籍、日和見主義、故郷** |

☐ 議論の内容を読んだあと、誰の意見に最も賛同しますか。
☐ あなたは鄭大世選手がどの国の代表選手になるべきだと思いますか。
☐ スポーツ大会に参加するために国籍を変えることについてどう思いますか。

2〜4人のグループに分かれて次の作業を行ってみましょう。

あなたのアイデンティティをパスポートや国籍以外の方法で理解するために、あなたを適切に表していると思うモノやシンボル、イメージなどをリストアップしてみてください。人種や宗教、ジェンダー、言語、家族などについて考える必要があるでしょう。これらが人のアイデンティティを形成する上でどのような影響を及ぼしているのかについて考えてみましょう。

リストづくりが終わったら、グループのメンバーたちと、なぜそれらを選んだのか話し合ってみましょう。その作業を通じて、リストから削除したいもの、またはリストに追加したいものはありましたか。

ケーススタディ 5
歴史は苦手

「今日が何の日か知っている人？」
　山下先生は学生たちに大きな声でプレッシャーをかけた。
「そうです。今日は、サプライズのミニ・テストを行う日です！　これから、日本史と関連した20問のクイズ形式のテストを実施しますので、皆さんの思考のスイッチをオンにしてくださいね」
　クラス一同は「エーッ」という嘆きの声を上げたが、山下先生はそれを気に留めず、学生たちを刺激し続けた。
「そうだ、ハナもご心配なく。今日のクイズには日本と朝鮮半島の関係も含まれているから、ハナにとってもそれほど難しくないはず」
　ハナは、またもや山下先生のミニ・テストで不合格になるかと思って、早くも滅入っていた。ハナの様子に気づいた由美は「ハナ、きっと大丈夫よ」と励ました。
「由美、私が歴史が苦手なのはわかるでしょ。もとから歴史の勉強は退屈だと思っていたし、日本に来て間もないから日本と関係する部分なんてわかるはずないわ。だから月曜日の午前にある歴史の授業は本当に苦痛なの」とハナは机にグッタリもたれながら答えた。
「いつも、同じ調子なの……。先生は皆に難しい質問を出して、それを私に答えさせる気がするのよ。まったく答えられない私ってバカみたい、といつも感じちゃうの」
　ハナは不満を吐露し続けた。
「ハナのその苦労は、私も十分理解できるわ」と由美はハナの様子を見ながら慰めた。
「韓国から来たから日本史で苦労するのは当然よね。しかも朝鮮半島の歴史も南北コリアで教え方が随分と違うと聞いているし。朝鮮戦争一つにしてもその原因からまったく違う教え方をしていると聞いたわ」
「私が学んだ歴史の授業では日本についての記述はどちらかといえば否定的なものだったのよ。だって、朝鮮半島は植民化されたんだから、中立とか客観とかという言葉で歴史を扱うには無理があって当然かもね。視点がどうしても異なるのよ」
　ハナがため息をつきながら言った。
「慰めにはならないかもしれないけど、私も歴史が一番苦手よ。うちの両親は、歴史なんてフィクションみたいなものだから心配しなくてもいいと言ってくれているわ。両親は、国の歴史だけを教えることが国際関係をこじらせると考えているみたい。だ

から共通のアジア史とか国内の郷土史や家族史などについても教えたり調べたりする授業が必要だと教えてくれたのよ」

　ハナは由美に向かって軽く微笑んだ。歴史なんて誰かがこしらえた物語に過ぎない、と彼女も思いたかった。しかし、その思いだけでは山下先生が行うミニ・テストの苦痛から逃れることにはならなかった。ハナは、故郷や在日コリアンの歴史の授業であればもっと自分のことを知ることができるし、みんなにもコリアンのことを知ってもらえると思った。月曜日に行われるミニ・テストのプレッシャーのために、ハナは歴史科目が苦手なままだった。

キーワード　**国家の歴史と地域や家族やマイノリティの歴史、事実とフィクション**

ディスカッション
- □ 共通のアジアの歴史を教える教科書を作ることは可能だと思いますか。
- □ 立場の違いによって歴史認識はどのような違いが生まれてくるのか例をあげて話し合ってみましょう。
- □ 地域やふるさと、家族レベルの歴史が大切な理由はなぜでしょう。同じ地域内でも対立する歴史を探し、その例と理由などについて話し合ってみましょう。
- □ あなたは歴史を「真実」だと思いますか。それとも「こしらえられた」物語だと思いますか。あなたの見解を明らかにしてその根拠を示してみましょう。

ケーススタディ 6
ハナが民族（朝鮮）学校に行く

　ハナは、在日コリアン 3 世であるヒャンミという他校の友人が初めてできたので、そのことがとても嬉しかった。二人は日本のある NGO が主催した、インターナショナル・スクールに通う学生のための多文化共生イベントで知り合った。
　「私は日本生まれで日本育ち。けれども朝鮮半島全体が私の祖国だと思っているわ。だから私は朝鮮籍のままなの」
　ヒャンミは自信あふれる口調で、流ちょうな朝鮮語でハナに告げた。彼女の堂々とした姿にハナは驚いた。
　「北朝鮮についてはどのように思うの？」
　ハナは勇気を出して聞いてみた。
　「そうね、確かに北朝鮮の政権には問題が多いわよね」
　ヒャンミはそう言って続けた。
　「でも私はコリアンであるから北朝鮮も韓国も祖国とか故郷だと思っているのよ。ところで、うちの学校で次の日曜日にオープン・スクール企画があるんだけど来てみない？」
　当初ハナは北朝鮮と関わりのある学校を訪ねることをためらった。ハナにとってみれば北朝鮮とのつながりがある朝鮮学校に行くことには、言葉で表せない感情があるからだ。もしも、自分の正体がばれてしまったら……、という不安を抱き、ハナが警戒心を強めることは不思議ではない。でもヒャンミにとても好感がもてたし、不安ながらも朝鮮学校の様子を見てみたいという好奇心が湧いてきたので、ハナは勇気を出して訪ねることにした。
　次の日曜日にヒャンミは、白と黒のチョゴリの制服姿で、ハナを学校の正門で迎えてくれた。他にも日本の学校の人たちが訪問しているのを見て、ハナの緊張も和らいだ。訪問者は日本語を話していたが、あわただしく準備に追われていた学生たちは朝鮮語を話していた。ゲストを迎えるときには「アンニョンハシムニカ？」という朝鮮語で迎えていた。
　ヒャンミがハナをホールの席に案内してから間もなくコンサートが始まった。中級部と高級部の学生たちが伝統的な楽器を演奏したり、歌や踊りを披露した。彼らの見事な演奏から、日ごろからよく練習していることが伝わってきたし、ハナは生徒たちの実力にも驚いた。そして、学生たちが演奏する姿を見て、北朝鮮に暮らしていた時

の学校生活のいろんな場面を思い出した。歌や踊りのスタイルは北朝鮮のそれと、さほど違いがなかったために、懐かしくも思えた反面、同時に複雑な気持ちにもなった。
「どうだった？」
　ヒャンミが感想を求めた。
「とても素敵だったわ」とハナが応えた。
「見て、みんなのってきたわ。保護者達も楽しんでいる」
　ハナは壇上に上がって踊りだした保護者を指しながらそう言った。
　午後には、朝鮮学校の「一日体験」が始まった。その時ハナはまた驚いた。学校の中を見回してみると、民族的なアイデンティティを表すたくさんの絵や標語のポスターがあり、そこには北朝鮮とのつながりがある内容、北朝鮮式の表現があったからだ。
「北朝鮮の色彩が強いとは思わないの？」とハナはヒャンミに聞いてみた。
「そうね、北朝鮮はこの学校を作るのを支えたという意味では重要な意味を持つわね。このあいだ言った通り、北朝鮮も韓国も、私たちにとっては祖国であり故郷なのよ。それが朝鮮学校で教育を受ける在日コリアンたちの共通の思いかもしれないわ」
「へ〜え、そうなんだ」
　ハナは話をそらすかのようにそう答えた。それ以上北朝鮮のことは何も聞けなかったので、話題を変えた。
「ところで教室では朝鮮語を話すの？」
「そうよ。日本語は学校の外で使っている。そして英語も習っているのよ」
　イベントの最後にキム校長先生が来訪者たちに感謝の辞を述べた。彼の話を通じて、朝鮮学校がおかれている厳しい状況が伝わってきた。なかでも、日朝間の関係悪化が高校授業料無償化措置への影響につながったことにも触れた。
「本日のように、地域との望ましい関係づくりを通じて、日本社会と在日朝鮮人の冷え切った関係を克服することができるでしょう」と深くお辞儀をしながら校長先生は来賓に挨拶した。
「ヒャンミ、今日は特別な日だったわ」とハナは別れ際に御礼を言った。
「楽しんでもらえてよかったわ。もっと多くの人があなたのように心を開いてくれると嬉しいのだけど。韓国からの訪問者に学校を見せることができて光栄よ」

ハナにハグをしながらヒャンミは言った。ハナは、何も言わずに黙っていた。
「急に静かになったね、どうかしたの、ハナ？」
「いいえ、何も。とても楽しかったわ。また近々会いましょうね」
　ハナはヒャンミに真実を告げるには、まだ時が早いことに気づき微笑んだ。
　家に戻ってからハナは改めて、勇気を出して朝鮮学校を訪問したことを振り返ってみた。言葉で上手に表せない北朝鮮でのたくさんの記憶や出来事を思い出す一日であった。と同時に、ハナはいろいろと不安が募ってしまった。

キーワード　韓国語、朝鮮語、コリア語、ハングル、韓国人、朝鮮人、コリアン、多文化主義、民族教育、日本のマイノリティ

アクティビティ

　2～4人のグループに分かれて次の作業を行いましょう。
☐ 日本にある朝鮮学校について調べてみましょう。朝鮮学校についてどのような印象を受けましたか。
☐ なぜ日本政府は朝鮮学校に対する補助を打ち切ったと考えますか。
☐ なぜ民族教育は必要だと思いますか。あなたの意見を述べてください。
☐ 朝鮮学校を訪問することからハナは何を学んだと思いますか。あなたはそのような学校を訪ねてみたいと思いますか。
☐ なぜ、NHKでは「ハングル講座」と言っていると思いますか。韓国語、朝鮮語、コリア語、韓国・朝鮮語などの表現の使い分けについて調べてみましょう。

ケーススタディ 7
ヘイトクライム

　ハナの毎朝の日課はコンピューターの電源を入れて密かに続けているブログを更新し、ブログへのコメント欄に目を通すことである。日本に暮らす若い脱北者の生活をつづる珍しいブログなので、アクセス数も日々増加し、ブログに残された応援メッセージや質問を読むことが楽しみになりつつあった。それでもハナは自身の個人情報が特定されないようにいつも注意を払い続けていた。それは何よりも、クラスメイトが偶然にでもこのブログを見つけ、書き手がハナでないかと勘ぐられることを恐れたからだ。
　ある日、いつものようにブログにアクセスしたハナは、記事の末尾にあるコメントの書き込みを見て凍り付いてしまった。
「いったいこれは何なの？」
　彼女の眼はびっくりしてまん丸になっていた。

「韓国・朝鮮人は死ね！」
「北朝鮮人は日本に来るな！」
「外国人お断り！　我々は犯罪者予備軍を必要としない！」
「ジャパニーズ・オンリー！」

　こんな攻撃的なメッセージが並んでいたのである。
　ハナは衝撃を覚え、よろめいてしまった。
「どうして？　何なのこれは？」
　ハナの身体は恐怖に震えていた。いくらなんでもひどすぎる。しばらくの間、茫然としていたハナは、はっと我に戻った。ヒャンミとの待ち合わせに遅れる寸前であることに気付いたのである。あわてて着替えて、ヒャンミに会うために猛ダッシュで家を飛び出した。
　ハナとヒャンミは知り合ってからまだそれほど時間が経っていないし、二人は異なる学校に通っているけれど、ここ数週間、毎朝合流して途中まで一緒に通学していた。二人は意気投合する仲になりつつあったが、ハナはヒャンミのあることが気になっていた。それは、ハナが朝鮮学校に訪ねた時にはヒャンミはチマチョゴリの制服姿だったのに、学校の外で会うときにはなぜか、一般的な制服と変わらない姿で現れるからである。今日は、ブログのこともあったので、もしかしてと思いその理由について聞いてみること

にした。
「ヒャンミ、少し、込み入った質問をしてもいいかしら？」
　ヒャンミは微笑みながらうなずいた。
「とても聞きづらいことを聞くけれど、ヒャンミの制服がチマチョゴリではないのは、もしかして最近のヘイトスピーチとかと関連しているの？　ごめん、答えにくかったら答えなくてもいいのよ」
　ヒャンミは一瞬戸惑った様子ではあったが、静かに喋り出した。
「これは第二制服と呼ばれるものなのよ。そうよ、ハナの想像は的中しているわ。これには悲しい現実があってね」
　そう話すヒャンミの目は少し悲しそうに見えた。
「チョゴリと関連してどのような悲しい話があったの？　教えてくれる？」
「要はね、チマチョゴリを着ることが心配なのよ。チョゴリを着ていたら私たちがコリアンであることは一目瞭然でしょ。それでヘイトクライムのターゲットになってしまうかもしれないのよ。だから身の安全のためにこの普通の制服を着ているの」
　朝鮮学校方面に向かいながら、過去に朝鮮学校の女子高生たちのチョゴリがカッター・ナイフで切られた事件があったことについてヒャンミは話してくれた。そして最近のヘイトクライムについても色々と話してくれた。
「ねえ、ヒャンミ。私、オンラインでヘイトスピーチとかヘイトクライムと関係するようなひどい書き込みを見つけたの」
　ハナは自らが被害者であることを伏せたまま書き込みについて説明した。それを聞いたヒャンミには特に驚く様子もなかった。
「それはよくあるヘイトスピーチの書き込みね、ハナ。それについてハナにできることは何もないかもしれないわ。どの国にもそういう心ない排外主義者がいるものなのよ」
　ハナは混乱した。すべてが不可思議に思えた。日本のような法治国家でなぜこれが放置されているのだろうかと。ヒャンミの学校に近づいたため二人は別れた。ハナは一人で「地球市民学校」に向かいながら考え続けた。

キーワード

**ヘイトクライム、ヘイトスピーチ、民族差別、
外国人排斥運動（ゼノフォビア）**

アクティビティ

　2～4人でグループを形成し次の質問について話し合ってから回答を作成してください。

☐ 在日コリアンは日本におけるもっとも古いマイノリティ集団の一つですが、なぜヘイトクライムなどの被害にあうのでしょうか。

☐ 政府がヘイトクライムを止めるべきでしょうか。これらを防ぐためにやるべきことは何ですか。

ケーススタディ 8
山下先生が
秘密を漏らしそうになってしまった

　ハナはいまだ学校での新生活に十分になじめず、色々と苦労をしていた。今日も彼女は授業に遅刻しそうになり、教室に入る山下先生の後を追いかける形で教室にギリギリでたどり着いた。ハナは英語の宿題をするのをうっかり忘れてしまっていた。ハナが大きなストレスを感じているのは、修学旅行で韓国に行く日が近づいていることに対してだった。
「気にするなよ、山下先生はみんなに厳しい人だから……。宿題は昼休みに僕と一緒にやれば問題ないさ」とアーロンはハナを元気づけた。
「ありがとう、アーロン。とても優しいのね」とハナは微笑んだ。
「友だち同士であたりまえじゃないかよ。ハナは夏休みの韓国への修学旅行を、すごく楽しみにしているんじゃないの？」
「いや〜ぁ、そうでもないのよ」
　実はハナは、韓国行きの旅行で自分の正体がばれてしまうのではないかと、不安な日々を過ごしていた。
「ハナにいろいろと案内してもらうからね」と、何も知らずに無邪気に話すアーロン。
　深呼吸を数回したら、ハナの気分は少し和らいだ。「地球市民学校」での生活が始まって以来、たくさんではないけれど、アーロンのような親切な友人も増えた。そんな時、山下先生の声が聞こえてきた。
「はい、皆さんよろしいですか。今週末に博物館へ現場学習に出かけることを忘れないでくださいね。各自お弁当を持参ですし、先日配った学習用紙も必ず持ってきてください。それから、現地集合ですので、遅れないように時間を厳守してください。それからハナ、地下鉄の乗り方についてはもう慣れたかな？　ちなみにピョンヤンの地下鉄に乗ったことはあるのかな？」
　先生のこの一言でハナは背筋が凍り付いてしまった。またクラスも一気に静まり返って全員がハナのほうを見ているような気がした。皆が何かコソコソささやいているようにも感じた。
「特に問題ありません、私だってもう、日本の電車の乗り換えくらいはできますよ。先生、ピョンヤンの地下鉄には南北コリアの統一後にぜひ乗ってみたいです」
　あわてたハナは臨機応変に答えた。
　一人のクラスメイトがクスクスと笑ったことで、山下先生も自分のミスに気付いた。

「そうだったね、いつかみんなでピョンヤンの地下鉄に乗りながら現場学習が自由にできる時代が来ればいいですね」

　何事もなかったように装ったつもりだが、ハナの顔は真っ赤に赤面し、顔を上げることができなかった。危なかった。山下先生がうっかり彼女の秘密をみんなの前で漏らしてしまいそうになった危機一髪のハプニングであった。一日中彼女は誰とも話さなかった。クラスメイトが「ちなみにピョンヤンの地下鉄には乗ったことがあるのかな？」という先生のセリフを繰り返し真似している幻聴が聞こえてきた。

　少し気晴らしが必要であると思い、放課後ハナはバスに乗ってお気に入りの韓国・朝鮮料理の食堂に出かけた。オーナーのリさんは在日コリアンで韓国・朝鮮語にも流暢である。リさんは北朝鮮からの帰国脱北者をサポートするNGOでボランティア活動をしていて、そこでハナと出会った。次第に、ハナの良き相談相手になった。

「リさん、今日はとても辛い一日だったの。だからリさんがつくる最高のビビンパが食べたくなったんです」

　ハナは窓際の席に座ってからそう弱音をはいた。

「今すぐつくってあげるわ。でもとても辛そうね。ハナ、何があったの？」

「山下先生がクラスメイトの前で私が北朝鮮から来たことをばらしそうになったの。すべてが台無しになるところだったんです」

「もし山下先生がばらしてしまったとしても、そんなに大変かしら？　いつかはちゃんと伝えたほうが良いと思うわよ」

　リさんはそうアドバイスした。

「きっとみんなビックリするわ。絶交されちゃうかもしれないし、独りぼっちになっちゃうかも。だって、北朝鮮の人間にどう接したらいいのか、みんなまったく考えたこともないに違いないもん。私は普通の人間だけど、その状況から逃げられないわ」

　ハナはもっと落ち込んだ表情でそう言った。

「かわいそうに。でも北朝鮮が貧しかったり、北朝鮮の政権に問題があったりすることがハナの責任ではないでしょ。ハナが本当のことを話す準備ができたら、たぶん話すことができるはず。みんなちゃんと耳を傾けてくれるわよ」

　リさんはニッコリと笑って、ハナの背中をやさしくさすってからゆっくりと厨房へ入っていった。

「たぶんリさんの言う通りかも、きっと」
　ハナは自分にそう言い聞かせた。

キーワード　コミュニティ、アイデンティティ、社会適応、カミングアウト

ディスカッション
- なぜ、ハナは彼女の過去が知られるのを怖がっているのでしょうか。
- あなたは、山下先生がハナの秘密について隠し通す責任があると思いますか。

アクティビティ
　世の中には様々な「アイデンティティ」があります。人びとのアイデンティティは応援するスポーツチームや好みのパソコンメーカー、そして支持する政党などさまざまに分かれます。
　あなたが自分について思うアイデンティティと他人があなたについて思うアイデンティティはどのような違いがあるのかを考えてみましょう。あなたが自分について思うアイデンティティをリストアップして、次に、他人があなたをどのように思っているのかについてもリストアップしてみましょう。周囲の人々とお互いのリストを比べてみましょう。

ケーススタディ 9
伝統文化それとも殺戮？

　昼休みが終わっても、いまだハナは気持ちを落ち着かせることができなかった。なぜなら、昼休みの間に日本人の卓也とカナダから来たアーロンの間で突発的なケンカが起きてしまったからである。このようなトラブルは些細な誤解や文化的な違いから何回か発生していた。
　いつものように卓也はお弁当のおかずとして魚介類の缶詰めを持ってきた。その缶詰めのラベルには「キング・オブ・シーフード」と書かれていた。ハナもアーロンもいまだ日本の料理文化には詳しくないため、それほど深く考えずに卓也が分けてくれた缶詰をおいしく食べた。
「これおいしいね、卓也」
　ハナは喜んだ。
「こんな変わったシーチキンは初めて食べてみるわ」
「シーチキン？　違う違う、これはクジラ肉だよ!!」と卓也が何気なく答えた。
　卓也の言葉にハナは特に驚かなかったが、すぐにアーロンの顔色が変わっていることに気づいた。
「な、なんだと？　マジか卓也？　クジラを食うなんて、お前正気か？　クジラの体内には多くの水銀がたまっているから人体に悪いんだぜ」
　アーロンは信じられないかのようにブツブツと文句を言いはじめた。
「俺たちによくもこんなもん食わしたな？　クジラ肉を食うなんてどうにかしているさ。吐き気がするよ。オウェ〜ッ、お前さんのことが信じられないぜ」
「おい、ちょっと待てよ、アーロン」
　卓也が反論し始めた。
「それは文化的な誤解に過ぎないんじゃないか？　僕は君がクジラ肉が苦手なんて思いもしなかったし、さらに国によって食文化は当然違うじゃないか。捕鯨問題だって、国によって立場が違う。それに禁止国の多くはかつてクジラ漁を行っていたんだぜ。韓国では犬を食べるし、フランスではカタツムリだって食うぜ。そんな堅苦しいこと言うなよ」
　卓也はアーロンの態度に明らかに怒っていた。
　ハナは何も言わず、ただ静かに黙っていた。本音を言うと、クジラ肉をとてもおいしいと思ったし、過去に犬の肉だって食べたことがある。カタツムリを食べたいと思っ

たことはなくても、卓也の指摘する食文化の違いについては十分理解できた。その一方で、多くのクジラが絶滅の危機にある動物であることも知っていた。

　アーロンも卓也も一歩も自分の考え方を譲ろうとしないために、状況は悪化していった。騒ぎを聞いていた担任の山下先生は隣に座り、「君たち、先生が思うに、二人とも半分は正しく、もう半分は偏見に満ちている。問題を正しく理解するためにも知的なディベートをすることで解決してみよう。せっかくだから楽しいやり方で進めましょう！」

　山下先生はニッコリと笑ってそう言った。
「アーロン、君はクジラやイルカを食べることを肯定する側になる。そして卓也は否定する側に回る。君たちのチームの役割はお互いを論破することだ、分かったな？残りの議論は明日の授業で続けることにしよう。グッドラック！」

　山下先生はそう言いつつ飲みかけのコーヒーを片手に教員室へと去って行った。
「自分の意見や立場を正反対に変えることなんてできるのかしら？」

　ハナは帰宅途中、ディベートのことを考え続けた。ディベートに積極的に参加できるよう、ハナは調査捕鯨の問題とイルカ漁のあり方について調べ始めた。

キーワード　食文化、伝統、道徳や倫理、異文化

ディスカッション
- □ もしもあなたがハナであれば、どちらの立場を取りますか。
- □ あなたの立場はどのように正当化されるでしょうか。
- □ 犬やカタツムリを食べることをどう思いますか。
- □ ペットと家畜を線引きすることはできますか。
- □ 動物園や水族館についてはどのように思いますか。

アクティビティ
　映画『ザ・コーヴ』を鑑賞後、2つのグループAとグループBに分かれてください。
　グループAの役割は太地町の人びとの文化を支持することです。
　グループBの役割は、太地町のイルカ漁は不要かつ残酷な殺戮であり、伝統の領域を遥かに超えていると捉えることです。

ケーススタディ 10
韓国人とコリアンは同じ事なの？

　新学期が始まってからすでに3か月近くが経過している。ハナの大阪での新しい学校生活は毎日が充実しており、国際色豊かなクラスメイトを通じて今まで知ることのなかった新しいことをハナは日々たくさん学んでいる。
　ある日の放課後、ハナはインホと雑談をしながら帰宅の準備をしていた。「地球市民学校」での生活に慣れていく中でハナはインホと親しくなった。彼は在日コリアンであったので、ハナも両親が在日コリアンのバックグランドについて話してくれたことを思い出して、インホとの繋がりを感じていた。
　学校から帰ろうとしていた時に、韓国人留学生会の執行部であるジュンホとチョルがハナのところへやってきた。ハナは不吉な予感がした。ジュンホは良い子だけど、クラスメイトたちの評判は正直いまひとつである。なぜならば、出身地が異なるクラスメイトたちの文化や風習に対しての配慮が少し足りないのである。まして、ジュンホは在日のキムチはニセモノキムチとまで言いふらしているという噂も聞いた。ハナが見る限り、ジュンホは韓国人以外の生徒とはそれほど付き合おうともしないし、また韓国語が分からない人の前でも平気で韓国語だけでしゃべり続ける。一方チョルはそうでもなく、誰とでも仲良く過ごしていた。二人がいつも一緒にいることが残念だとハナは思った。
「ハナ、ちょっと話があるんだけどさ……」
　ハナが最後の教科書をカバンに入れようとした時にジュンホが声をかけてきた。
「ねえ、君は僕たちのことを意図的に避けているような気がするんだけど、違うかな……。たまに僕らと話すときも韓国語では話しかけてくれないじゃないか。それに、僕たちが執行部を務めている韓国人留学生会の活動にもまったく顔を出してくれないし。一度参加してくれるとありがたいんだけどなぁ」
「別に、避けているつもりはなかったけど。でも、なかなか参加できなくてゴメンね」
　ハナは戸惑いながら答えた。
「今度行けたら行くね。でも、最近いろんなことで立て込んでいるのでちょっと忙しいの……。もし次回も行けなかったら許して。ゴメン」
　彼女は目線をそらしながら答えた。
「別に大丈夫だよ」
　励ますかの如くチョルが言った。するとジュンホが「僕たちはハナが参加してみん

なともっと親しくなってほしいと思っているのさ。こんなこと余計なお世話かもしれないけどさぁ、もしかして、君は訛りを気にしすぎているんじゃないの、ハナ？　俺たち別に、訛りとか方言なんか気にしてないよ。大丈夫だって。君の韓国語の発音を聞く限り、ハナ、君は江原道あたりの出身だよね。うちのじいちゃんと訛りがそっくりだ！」
　さらにジュンホが続ける。
「そんなの誰も気にしないさ。俺たちみんな大韓民国の仲間じゃなか！　今度一緒にサッカー韓日戦の応援に行こう。そこでみんなでテーハンミグッ！　て叫びながら応援しようよ。特に日本では僕たちの歴史や文化も守らなければいけないしね」
　インホはハナのほうを見つめて、ジュンホが言ったことに不愉快な表情を浮かべた。「なんでもかんでも大韓民国って物言いは、いかがなものかなぁ」と言いたげな表情であった。
「サッカーの応援もそうだけど次回の会合にぜひ参加してね」
　ジュンホが促してきた。
「僕たち、今度の学園祭でいくつかの企画を準備しているんだ」
「う〜ん、頑張ってみるね。でも、確約はできない、許して」
　ハナは力なく答えた。
「あっそうだ、バスに乗り遅れちゃう。また明日ね」と言いつつハナはその場から逃げ去った。

キーワード　包摂、排除、我が民族、ナショナリズム

ディスカッション
- 何故、ハナはジュンホとチョルの二人と距離を置いてきたのでしょうか。
- あなたもハナのように他人と意図的に距離を置いたりした経験がありますか。
- ジュンホは韓国を愛する愛国者みたいですが、それがハナの不愉快さの原因みたいですね。国を愛することはいけないのでしょうか。

アクティビティ

2～4人のグループに分かれて、次の点について話し合って答えを準備してください。

皆さんは「私たち（We/Us）」と「彼ら・奴ら（They/Them）」といった自己と他者を、いつ、誰と、そしてどのような場面で線引きしますか。話し合ってみましょう。

このような用語を使った結果、誰が利益を得て、誰が不利益を被るのでしょうか？

ディベートを開始する前に、あなたのグループの主張すべき点についてまとめてみましょう。国際社会、南北コリア、日本の視点を網羅するようにしてください。

ケーススタディ 11
ハナが西日本入国管理局に行く

　太陽が高くのぼりかけたある日のお昼前、大阪郊外にある西日本入国管理局の近くのバス停に停まったバスから降りる人びとの中にハナの姿が見える。ハナは難民支援NGOの体験ボランティア活動に参加することになった。今日がその初日であり、早速、不法滞在などを理由に拘束、収監されている外国人への面談に同行することになったのである。ハナの役割は、当事者と会って話を聞くことである。特に、中国籍朝鮮族の趙(チョウ)さんという女性とは朝鮮語で話してほしいと、NGOのスタッフに頼まれていた。
「西日本入国管理局へようこそ」
　職員がハナたちを迎えてくれた。
「今日の体験ボランティアが有益になることを願っています。そしてボランティアの今日のお仕事は二人の拘留者に会って、彼らの話を聞いてあげることです。彼らにとって誰かが訪ねてきてくれたり、話を聞いてくれたりすることは大きな力になります」
　ハナは緊張気味の表情で微笑み、職員の後を追ってセキュリティ・チェックを通過し、面談室へと入っていった。
「へ〜え、思った以上に普通なんだぁ」とハナは内心驚いた。
「ここは高級ホテルとは言えませんが、それでも拘留者に快適な環境を与えようとしています」と入管職員は言った。
　ハナを案内した職員は一旦席を外し、一人の外国人と一緒に戻ってきた。この人は50歳代初めに見える男性で、アリ・ウェラットさんという名だった。大きな体格の彼は、やつれた顔つきにとても大きな手をしていて、指を頻繁にならしていた。最初に彼が自己紹介をしてから事情を話してくれた。
「私はここにすでに2か月もいます。私はトルコ系のクルド人です。皆さんはクルド人の悲しい現実についてすでにご存じだと思います。日本が大変住みやすい国であると友人から聞いて、日本に来ました。貯金を使って日本に来るチケットを購入しました。最初は出稼ぎ労働をしていましたが、そうするうちに、学生時代に私がクルド民族の独立を掲げるグループに所属していたことが政府に知られて問題となったという連絡をトルコにいる友人から受けました。それですぐに難民申請を行いました。けれども日本政府はそれを認めてくれそうにないのです。何が起きるかとても不安です。トルコに強制退去させられたら、私はいったいどうなることやら……。トルコ政府は私を迫害するかもしれず不安です」

彼の声は震えていた。
「一番大きな問題は、私が本当にクルド独立運動にかかわっていた具体的な証拠がなく、トルコに送還されても迫害されないだろうと考えている日本政府の立場です。もしもトルコに強制送還されたら、むしろ目立ってしまい、結果的に迫害される可能性が大きいのです。しかし、日本政府はそのことにはまったく配慮してくれません。私は日本が好きです。もしも日本で暮らせるのであれば、建設現場で働きながら静かに暮らします。私は問題など絶対に起こしません。今後何が起きるかわかりませんが、この国で暮らしたいのです」

アリさんとの面談を終えて、今度は40歳代初めの女性の趙さんとの面談が始まった。顔にやけどの傷跡が少し目立つ人である。やさしくハナと握手を交わし、趙さんはハナの訪問に感謝を告げた。趙さんは朝鮮語で彼女の境遇を話してくれた。
「私は中国の東北地方出身で、もう8年も日本に住んでいます。ここで不法滞在をしつつ、あるレストランの厨房で働いていました。私は今年の初めに警察に捕まって入管の施設に送られました。私には幼い女の子の赤ちゃんがいます。その子のお父さんは日本人です。でも結婚しているわけではありません。こんな事情で日本に滞在できるのかどうかはわかりません。法務省には娘と共に暮らせるように特別在留許可を求めています。あの子の未来が心配です。娘にはお母さんが必要なんです」
趙さんはハナに赤ちゃんの父親と連絡をとって、赤ちゃんの近況を教えてもらえな

いかと頼んだ。ハナは、アリさんや趙さんがより良い暮らしを求めて日本に来たことを学んだ。彼らのことを哀れに思いながらも、だからと言って不法滞在が許されるべきなのかどうかについては答えがみつからなかった。

入管の施設から外に出たハナは、建物の方を振り返って、「ここにいる誰もが悲しいストーリーをもっているのだから、日本が難民や外国人にもう少し寛大になってくれればいいのに……」と思った。

キーワード　入国管理局、不法滞在、迫害、避難

ディスカッション
- アリさんは日本での滞在が認められるべきだと思いますか。もしそうでないとしたら彼はどこに送られるべきなのですか。
- 趙さんは日本での滞在が認められるべきだと思いますか。もしそうでないとしたら、彼女はどこに送られるべきですか。
- あなたは二人のような人びとを助けるNGOについてどう思いますか。
- 日本は難民や外国人の受け入れ政策に消極的な側面があります。上記のように日本に長年暮らしていて、また家族や子どもがいる場合、人道的な側面に照らしてみた場合、在留許可を与えるべきなのでしょうか、それとも退去命令を出すべきなのでしょうか。

アクティビティ
2～4名のグループに分かれて、アリさんや趙さんの日本における滞在が許されるべき、または許されてはいけない理由について書き出してください。これらの項目を活用しつつ討論を始めてください。

ケーススタディ 12
ハナとアーロンの映画鑑賞

　ハナとアーロンは学校で忙しい一週間を過ごしたので、ちょっとした気晴らしが必要であると感じていた。アーロンはハナを、これから上映中の韓国映画『クロッシング』を観に行こうと誘った。ハナに見に行く気になってくれるよう、『クロッシング』のあらすじをメールで送った。

　映画のストーリーは、北朝鮮の鉱山で働く主人公が、病気になった奥さんの薬を求めて不法に中国に密入国することから始まる。妻と子供を北朝鮮に残したまま主人公は中国に渡ったが、妻は間もなく病死し、11歳の息子は父を探し求めて中国に渡る。『クロッシング』は1990年代半ばに北朝鮮で起きた100万人規模の餓死者をもたらしたともいわれる飢餓問題を描いている。食糧やより豊かな生活を求める北朝鮮の人びとは、南北の軍事境界線があるために直接韓国には行けない。したがって、脱北者は中国や東南アジアを経由して安全な場所を求める。『クロッシング』は決して過去の物語ではない。いまだに中国は、北朝鮮の人びとを難民として認めず、彼らを北朝鮮に送還してしまう。

　ハナはこのような話が映画化されていることを知って驚き、ぜひ一緒に観たいと伝え、映画館の前で午後7時にアーロンと会う約束をした。
　二人はポップコーンや炭酸飲料を片手に、暗い映画館の中に入り席に座った。間もなく照明が完全に落ち映画が始まった。アーロンはこの映画は涙腺が緩くなる映画なのでハンカチが必ず必要だと言っていたが、当初ハナはあまり気にしていなかった。しかし映画が始まるや否や、ハナの前で繰り広げられる脱北者一家のストーリーにハナは茫然と見入ってしまった。
　映画が終わり、再び照明が明るくなり、観客が劇場の外へと流れ出るころになっても、ハナは立ち上がることができなかった。アーロンは上映中はハナの様子に気づかなかったが、このとき彼女がこの映画に感激したことを確信した。軽くハナの肩をたたきながら「映画はどうだった？」と感想を聞いてみた。
　ハナは、ふと我に戻り、「すごい、脱北者をテーマにしたこんな映画があるなんて信じられない。とてもビックリしたし、本当に言葉が出ないわ。とてもリアルに描かれたストーリーだと思う。多くの人びとはいまだ定住先での生活に苦しんでいるわ」
　「そう、良かったね、感銘を受けたようで僕もうれしいよ。けれど、ハナが脱北者問

題にそれほど詳しいとは知らなかったなぁ〜。まるでテレビのコメンテーターみたいなコメントだね」

アーロンが冗談交じりで言った。

「韓国に多くの脱北者が定住するけれど、韓国での生活になじめずに、英国などの第三国に再移住する人が増えているみたいなのよ。そして日本にも脱北者が暮らしていると以前ある記事を読んだことがあるわ」

こう言うハナの表情はとても悲しそうであった。

「すごく遠くに行くんだね」

アーロンがそういった。

「そうよ、とても遠くにね」と、彼女の秘密について知るわけもないアーロンにそう言った。

キーワード　難民・避難民、無国籍者、脱走者、メディア

- 脱北者について知っている内容をもとに意見交換を行いましょう。なぜ、そのような人びとが存在すると思いますか。
- 彼らが今直面している問題とはどのようなものでしょうか。
- もしあなたが難民・避難民であり、故郷に帰れないとしたら、どうすると思いますか。
- あなたの社会が難民や難民申請者のためにできることは何だと思いますか。

2〜4名のグループに分かれて、あなたの国や外国の難民問題について話し合いましょう。

大衆文化やメディアの難民に対する姿勢はどのようなものだと思いますか。

どのような物語（コンフリクト、災害、政治抗争）が難民と関係していますか。

こういったことは人びとに難民に対するどのようなイメージを抱かせていると思いますか。

ケーススタディ 13
ハナの手紙

　ハナは時々ホームシックを感じるときがある。最近アーロンと映画を観に出かけてから、家のことや家族のことがさらに心配になった。難民支援を行う NGO からハナは、日本からも北朝鮮の家族に手紙や小包を送る方法があることを教えてもらった。
　NGO の担当者はハナに「もしも北朝鮮にいる家族に手紙を書くのであれば、脱北して日本に暮らすあなたからの連絡であることは隠さなければいけません。万一日本に暮らしていることを北朝鮮当局が知ったら、家族たちの身に危険が及ぶかもしれないからね。だから、ハナからの手紙とは書かずに、ちょっとした手がかりを書いて手紙の送り主があなたであることを知らせるのよ」
　この助言を肝に銘じて、ハナは火曜日の早朝にベッドから起き上がり机に向かい、ペンを取って両親への手紙を書き始めた。当局の検閲を恐れて、自分が母の日本に暮らす従妹であるという設定にした。

　　スクジャ姉さん、ドンヒョン義兄さん、

　何よりもこの手紙が無事届くことを願います。スクジャ姉さん、私は従妹のキョンオクです。私のことを覚えていますか。そう 8 月生まれのキョンオクです。イチゴ味のアイスが大好きで、左側の足首にあざがあるキョンオクと言えば、思い出してもらえるでしょうか。
　お姉さんと大阪で一緒に遊んでいたあの頃がもうずいぶんと前のことになってしまいましたね。
　お二人にお変わりはありませんか。お二人と最後に会ってからとてもとても長い時間がたってしまったようです。お姉さん夫婦に会いたい気持ちになるたびに、私の選択は誤ったのではないかと悔やんだりもします。お二人が背中を押してくださったので私はとても豊かな世界で生きていますが、お二人は私の選択をどのように思っていらっしゃるのでしょうか。そうですね、既に半世紀も前のことですから。私は日本でとても元気に過ごしています。一生懸命暮らしお金も稼ぎながら、私たちが望んでいた暮らしをするため頑張っています。
　そちらはお元気ですか。お二人にとても会いたいといつも思っていますが、偉大な祖国建設をするために一緒に帰国しなかったことを後悔したりする時もあり

ケーススタディ 13 ハナの手紙

ます。お二人は祖国で幸せに暮らしているのでしょうね。いつかお二人を訪ねてみたいと思ったりもします。

　スクジャ姉さん、お姉さんは今でも私たちが子どものころよく食べていた蒸しパンを作っているのでしょうか。今、そのパンがとても食べたいです。背中の痛みは少し和らいだでしょうか。別便で送る小包に薬を同封します。無事届くと良いのですが。そして、現金も少し送ります。そのお金で温かい服でも買って、寒い冬を凌いでください。

　スクジャ姉さん、お姉さんにとても会いたいです。お姉さんとドンヒョン義兄さんへの私の気持ちは全く揺らぎません。もし可能であればお正月を祝うときのために、家族写真を送ってください。この時期になるとお姉さんたちにとても会いたくなるのです。

　愛しています。

リ・キョンオクより

　翌日の放課後、ハナはあえて学校や家から離れた郵便局に向かった。まずは手紙を送り、そして後日送る小包に関する問い合わせをした。北朝鮮に手紙を送りたいというハナの言葉に、郵便局員は驚いた様子であった。慣れない様子の郵便局員は、いろいろな資料を読みながら、日本から北朝鮮に送れるもの、送れないものについて説明してくれた。北朝鮮に対する制裁が、普通の人びとに送る郵便物にまで影響していることを改めて知った。手紙が無事家族に届くか、心配でたまらない放課後であった。

キーワード 離散家族、移住、コミュニケーション手段

ディスカッション

□ ハナが日本に来たことは良かったと思いますか。
□ なぜハナは家族と今すぐ再会できないのでしょうか。
□ なぜハナは家族に実名で手紙を送らないように助言されたのでしょう。
□ ハナが、お正月に家族に会いたいと思う気持ちになるのはなぜだと思いますか。
□ あなたが難民であり、家族や友人と離ればなれであったとしましょう。そして、二度と家族と再会できないかもしれません。あなたは、故郷の何をもっとも恋しがり、どのような手紙を家族宛に書くと思いますか。

アクティビティ

　グループをつくって、人びとが故郷を去って他の地域に行く理由について書いてみましょう。この作業が終わったら、書き込んだ内容を以下のように分けてください。

　1）人びとが自発的に移住をする状況。
　2）人びとが強制的に移住を強いられる状況。

　2つのリストを活用してそれぞれの理由について議論してみたり、移住者と難民の境目について話し合ってみましょう。

　さらに、移住者が故郷に暮らす人びととどのように連絡を取り続けるか考えてみましょう。

　移住者たちは、どのような連携をつくりそれを維持するのでしょうか。

ケーススタディ 14
南北コリアの統一は必要？

「地球市民学校」では水曜日に討論会が定期的に開かれる。ハナはセミナー・ルームに入り、すでに部屋にいたみんなと挨拶をした。学生たちはランチを食べて空腹を満たしながら、討論のための資料をまとめていた。ハナと友人たちが一緒に集まって討論する今学期のシリーズ・テーマは、北東アジアの文化、社会問題、そして政治問題である。そして今週のテーマは、インホが提案した南北コリアの統一問題であった。

インホは洋服にこぼれ落ちたお菓子を払い落としてから討論を始めた。彼は南北コリアの統一はとても重要であり、また緊急な課題であると力説した。事前に準備したノートを活用しながら、在日コリアンは南北コリアが統一されることによってはじめて繁栄するのだという彼の持論を展開した。

韓国からの留学生であるジュンホは、インホの考え方には賛同しなかった。
「韓国人として言わせてもらうけれど、統一は韓国側が北朝鮮側を経済的に支えることになるので、韓国の次世代にとって南北統一は経済的な負担以外の何でもないのさ。インホ、君の考えは申し訳ないけど理想主義的なものに聞こえるね。でも実際に統一とは、経済的な負担や社会秩序の混乱など、現実問題から捉える必要があるんだ」

ジュンホがキッパリとそう言い切った。

チョルは多少躊躇しながらも次のように自分の意見を述べた。
「ジュンホ、僕は君とは少し意見が違うな。朝鮮半島の分断は確かに 70 年以上も続いているから固定化していて、韓国の負担は無視できない。けれど、数千年の歴史の流れから言えば、70 年の分断なんてたったほんのわずかな時間に過ぎないさ。統一はいつか実現するし、朝鮮半島の人びとや周辺諸国の人びとにとっても歓迎されることであると、僕は確信するよ」

情熱あふれる討論に中立的な立場を堅持していたアーロンは「国際社会は統一に先立って、北朝鮮の人権問題や貧困問題を解決できるのかな？」と疑問を投げかけた。

ジュンホは再びこれらの問題は韓国のみでは解決できるものではないと主張した。
「すでに 3 万人の脱北者が韓国にいることを知っているよね。たったこれだけの数の脱北者でもいろんな問題が韓国内で発生しているのに、2500 万人の北朝鮮人を支えるなんてことになったら、そんなのできるはずないさ」

「南北コリアの統一で、朝鮮半島の人口は 7000 万人以上になる。こうなれば経済的にも大国になれるかもしれない。だから統一は危機ではなくむしろチャンスだと思う

よ」とチョルが統一の必要性を韓国人の立場から繰り返した。
「どうやら韓国人同士でも、統一に関する意見は様々なようだね」と言うアーロン。
「僕が思うに、日本の視点からすると統一は歓迎できないな」
ハナの日本人のクラスメイトである卓也が言った。
「朝鮮半島の統一による不安定な国際政治を想像してみてごらんよ、それに南北が一緒になったら反日の勢いはますますエスカレートするかもね。そんな状況を見たくないな」
これが卓也の本音であった。
「離散家族問題はどうすれば良いのよ？」

ハナは沈黙を破って討論に参入した。
「長年の間、離れ離れの人びとが一緒にならなくてもいいの？　お金の問題がそんなにも重要なの？」
「ハナの言っていることは確かに正論だ」
　アーロンがそう言いながら続けた。
「でも、状況はそう簡単そうでもないね。結局大多数の人びとにとって、人道的な観点よりも経済的な問題のほうが重要なのさ。もっと考えるべきことがたくさんあるんだよ」
　ハナとインホはお互いを見つめては、がっかりしたかのように頭を横に振った。クラスメイトは、人道的配慮からこの統一問題をまったく捉えようとはしていないようであった。そんなときちょうど昼休みの終わりを知らせるチャイムが鳴った。
「よし、みんな、今日はここまでだね、来週また同じ時間に集まろう、いいかな？」とアーロンが取りまとめた。
　ハナは何も言わないまま、その場を静かに去っていった。

キーワード　**分断、統一、統一のコスト、人道的配慮**

ディスカッション
- あなたは、南北コリアの統一が実現可能だと思いますか。その理由はなぜですか。
- あなたは、南北コリアの統一に賛成ですか、反対ですか。その理由をあげてください。
- あなたは、国際社会の各メンバーが南北の統一と分断のどちらで利益を得ようとしていると思いますか。

アクティビティ
本当に統一が意味のあることなのか議論してみましょう。
　二つのグループに分かれて、一方は統一を支持し、もう一方は統一に反対する立場で議論してみてください。あなたたちの議論を始める前に、上であげた議論の争点やポイント（人道的観点、経済的観点、民族自決権など）をあげてみましょう。

ケーススタディ 15
転校生、彼女は何者？

ハナのクラスは、今日一人の学生が編入してくるというニュースでどよめいていた。山下先生が、転校生の女の子が1時間目の途中にやってくるとアナウンスしたのだ。ちょうど9時過ぎに誰かが教室のドアをノックした。いつもストライプ柄のスーツを着ているために「アル・カポネ」というあだ名がつけられている校長の木村先生とともに、ジーンズにTシャツ姿、そして赤い野球帽をかぶった女の子が入ってきた。木村先生は山下先生に何かをささやき、生徒たちの前に無表情で立っている彼女を一人残したまま教室から出ていった。

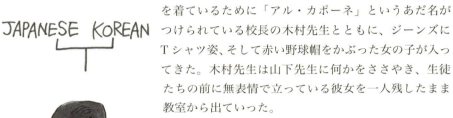

「皆さん、紹介します。すでにお知らせしているように、新しい仲間のマリコです」

山下先生がいつもの口調でアナウンスした。転校生は声を整えて話し始めた。

「よろしく、実はティナとよく呼ばれているので、ティナと呼んでね。私の英語名です」

「それなら、ティナと呼ぼう」

少しあわてた山下先生が答えた。

「では、あそこに座っているハナの隣に座ってください。彼女があなたをいろいろと手助けしてくれるはずです」

ティナはバッグを肩からおろし、ハナの隣にゆっくりと着席した。

「ようこそ、ティナ。私はハナ。実は私もこの学校に来てからそれほど長くはないけど、いろいろと教えてあげるわね。みんなと一緒にランチしない？」

「ありがとう、喜んで」

ハナの誘いにティナがそう応じた。

ハナはティナに学校のことをいろいろと紹介しつつ、ランチをしているクラスメイトたちの仲間に加わった。

「ティナ、よろしく。君はどこから来たの？ 君はアメリカ英語をしゃべるね。見る限り野球も好きそうだし……」
　卓也が根掘り葉掘り聞き始めた。
「でも外見からしてティナちゃんは純血の日本人だよね？」と質問した。
　ティナの表情はすぐさま硬直した。
「純血の日本人？ それって何？」
　ティナはがっかりしたかのように聞き返した。
「はっきり言うけど私のお父さんは日系アメリカ人で、母はコリアン・アメリカンよ。そして、私は今までの人生をアメリカや海外で過ごしてきたわ。あなたの物差しでいえばハーフってことね。そういうことが言いたいのね？」
「いやぁ、あいつはただ君が転校生だから好奇心から聞いてみただけじゃないかな、ティナ。今度学校の近くにあるアメリカン・スタイルのピザ屋にでも行こうよ」
　インホが仲裁するかのように言った。
「日本は長い歴史と世界中でもっとも優れた文化を持っている国だから、日本の文化に誇りを持ってね。君にも日本人の血が流れているんだからさ」
　卓也がふてくされたようにそう言い返した。
　卓也のこの発言で、周囲は一気に静まり返り、ティナの顔も真っ赤になってしまった。
「私はそのような偏見や差別体験を転校するたびに経験してきたわ。卓也君、あなたは両親が日本国籍だから自分が純血の日本人だと思っているんでしょ。そして、そのことが私よりも優れているとでも言いたいの？
　でも、私はアジア系のアメリカ人であることを誇りに思っているし、日本と朝鮮半島の両方をルーツに持

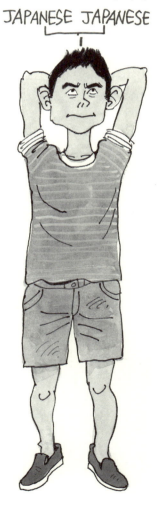
© Chung In-kyung

つことも嬉しいわ。それが私のすべてだし、それによって差別をする人をむしろ哀れに思う。お願いだから色眼鏡をかけて人を判断することはやめてほしいわね」
「そういうつもりではなかった。ごめん」
　譲らないティナの威勢に卓也も少し驚いたのか謝った。
「僕はただ日本の歴史と文化は誇りを持てるものだと言いたかっただけさ。僕の両親はいつも、日本の長い歴史と文化を誇りにしなさいと言っている。だからティナちゃんにもそのことを伝えたかっただけさ」
「それはどこの国でも同じじゃない？　むしろ私は日本と韓国、そしてアメリカの多様なバックグランドを持っていることが何よりも誇りよ。すでに３つの言語が自由自在だし、私は家族のおかげでグローバルな視点を持てたと信じているわ」
　怒りが収まらないティナが少しきつく言い続けた。
「怒らないで、ティナ。卓也君は日本の歴史と文化に誇りを感じているのはいいんだけど、異文化に対しては少し理解が足りないの。でもこの学校のほとんどの学生が多様なバックグランドを持っているのよ。みんなあなたの良い友だちになれるはずよ……」
　ハナがティナを落ち着かせようとした。
「私こそごめんなさい。そんなにカ〜ッとならなくても良かったはずなのに……。日本とか韓国に来ると何ていうか見世物扱いされている気がしちゃうので、つい……。卓也君、私も言い過ぎたわ。悪く思わないでね」
　彼女が卓也に謝った。
「これからもっとお互いについて学びましょう」
　これに卓也もニッコリと微笑み、ホッとしたみんなの表情が笑顔にもどった。

キーワード　ハーフ、ダブル、混血、同化、ステレオタイプ

ディスカッション
- □「純粋」とか「純血」という表現の何が問題なのでしょうか。
- □ なぜ「ハーフ」と「混血」という表現が、人びとを傷つけたりするのでしょうか。
- □ なぜクラスメイトはティナが「何人」であるかにこだわったのでしょうか。

ケーススタディ 16
ハナの秘密

　山下先生は机の後ろから学生たちを一瞬眺めてから「次はハナの発表の順番だね。前に出て、みんなのためにプレゼンテーションを始めてください」と大きな声で告げた。
　ハナは報告用のノートを片手に、教室の前にゆっくり歩み出てUSBメモリをプレゼンテーション用のノートパソコンに差し込んだ。震えるハナの手は「私の故郷」というファイルのアイコンの上にカーソルを乗せたが、そのファイルを開けることはためらった。彼女は大きく息を吸ってから話し始めた。
「皆さん、本来私の報告は在日コリアンについてのプレゼンテーションでしたが、昨夜とても大切なことに気が付き、急きょ少し内容を変更することにしました。私たちのクラスメイトは、みんなそれぞれ異なる背景を持ち、またお互い違いがあります。私たちはその違いを大切にすることを学んできました。私は今日のプレゼンテーションを通して、皆さんに隠していたことをお伝えしたいと思います」
　ハナの声は小さく震えていた。
　アーロンと由美はお互いの顔を見つめながら、ハナがいったい何を隠してきたのか、そしてこれから何が起きるのか、どんな秘密を隠していたのか、不可解な表情を浮かべた。
　ハナは再びカーソルをアイコンの上に置き、迷いなくダブルクリックした。明るくなったスクリーンには「私の故郷は、北朝鮮の新義州です」という言葉が浮かびあがった。そして、タイトルの下には笑顔の人びとに囲まれているハナが写っている写真があった。
「私は北朝鮮の新義州出身です。そしてここに写っているのは私の家族です。家族は今も北朝鮮に住んでいます」とプレゼンテーションを始めた。
　クラス中は一気に静まり返った。
「素晴らしい、ハナ。ぜひ私たちにその続きを聞かせてください」
　山下先生は椅子から立ち上がり、ハナを応援した。
「ガンバレ」
　アーロンが大きな声で叫んだ。
「続けて、ハナ！」
　ハナは再び深呼吸をしてから、次のスライドに進んだ。
「私は中朝国境近くの都市である新義州で生まれました。この写真にある通り綺麗な

山々があります。夏には家族とトウモロコシを川辺で焼いて食べたりしました。冬はとても寒いのですが市場で買い入れた石炭でオンドルという床暖房を焚いて寒さをしのぎました。池が凍ったら、そこで友だちとよくアイススケートをして遊んでいました。皆さんは北朝鮮がひどいところであると想像しているでしょうが、我が家の生活事情は1990年代の初期までは比較的裕福だったのです」

　ハナはマウスをクリックし、スクリーンに次のスライド資料を映し出した。その写真は、港で人びとが旗を振りながら大きな船に乗っている人びとに声をかけるものであった。

「我が家は1961年に日本から北朝鮮に、在日朝鮮人の帰国事業の一環として戻りました。両親はまだ子どもだったみたいです。北朝鮮に渡れば物質的にも豊かになり、日本で朝鮮人であるために受けた差別もなくなると考えたようです。北朝鮮に着いたら生活はかなりきつかったようですが、周囲には同じような帰国者が数多くいましたし、食べ物や石炭が不足してもお互いに協力し合っていたそうです」

　別の画面がスクリーンに現れた。

「我が家は1990年代後半から2000年代のはじめ、とても苦しい体験をしました。この時期は苦難の行軍と言われ、北朝鮮の普通の人びとは食べ物が不足していました」

　ハナは飢えで痩せ細った子どもの写真が写ったスクリーンを見ながら説明を続けた。

「人が飢え死にし、すべてが混乱する中で、両親は私の未来を案じて、私を中国に逃がしたのです。私は家族や友だちを残して離れたくありませんでした。私は故郷の山や川を離れたくありませんでしたが、そこに残っていたら生き残っていなかったかもしれません」

　ハナの声は震えていたが、熱心に聞くクラスメイトの姿に勇気を得て、中国の地図を見せながら話を続けた。

「私は故郷を離れ中国に不法入国し、そこでしばらく働いていました。しばらくして、もし中国の公安に見つかったら北朝鮮に強制送還されてしまうので、たいへん危険であることを知りました。幸い、脱北者を含む難民支援をする日本のNGOの助けを得て、最終的には日本の大使館関係者と接触し、その後、大阪に来ることができました」

　ハナは教室のほうを振り向いた。

「この話を隠し続けることがとても辛かったため、皆さんに伝えることにしました。

© Chung In-kyung

故郷の家族や友だち、そして故郷がとても恋しいです。日本にこうやって暮らすことは幸せですが、両親とともに暮らせないため、とても辛いです。最後までご清聴頂きありがとうございます。私の気もちが皆さんにうまく伝われば良いのですが……」
　アーロンと由美がリードしたクラスメイトたちの大きな拍手喝采がしばらくの間教室で鳴り響いた。
「ハナ、すごいわね」
　由美がハナを褒め称えた。
「もちろん君の思いは僕たちにちゃんと伝わったよ。ハナの故郷はとても美しく、ハナは家族に会いたいんだね。これからは何も隠す必要なんかないさ、僕たちは君が誰であろうが友だちなんだから」
　クラスが再び静かになった頃、山下先生が立ち上がりクラス全員を見つめた。
「今日はハナの故郷である北朝鮮の新義州について学びました。彼女の家族や友人が耐えなければいけなかった苦労についても学びました。なによりも皆さんにとって大切なのは、地球市民が何を意味し、人びとが北朝鮮人であろうが、日本人であろうが、カナダ人であろうが韓国人であろうが、あらゆる人びとにとって家族や故郷が大切であることを学んだということです」
　山下先生は引き続き生徒を眺めながら言った。
「私たちはハナ、あなたを誇りに思います。あなたの今日の報告はとても勇気のいることであり、担任の教師としてあなたを誇りに思います」
　ハナの真っ赤になった顔を卓也が見つけて「お〜い、ハナの頬っぺたが真っ赤だよ」とからかった。

キーワード　飢餓、離散、包摂と排除

ディスカッション
- ハナがクラスメイトに北朝鮮出身であることを隠してきた理由はなぜでしょうか。
- なぜ、ハナは秘密を公表しようとしたと思いますか。
- なぜ、難民たちには心の傷が残るのだと思いますか。
- 北朝鮮と北朝鮮難民（脱北者）について知っていることはありますか。あなたの知識は十分だと思いますか。

アクティビティ
2〜4人ごとにグループをつくり、次の作業を行いましょう。
ハナの秘密を聞いたら、あなたはどのように反応したでしょうか。
またなぜそのように思いましたか。グループ間で話し合ってみましょう。

エピローグ

　この教材は日本、韓国、オーストラリア、ニュージーランドの研究者たちの研究と情熱の産物であります。多様な背景を持つ人びとの移住、アイデンティティ、相互理解に焦点を合わせています。

　執筆者たちは主人公ハナが「地球市民学校」で学業をつづけ、大学にも進学することを想定しています。彼女は日本での定住生活で更なる試練を経験するでしょうが、「地球市民学校」での体験物語があらわしているように、周囲の人びとのサポートによって、それらを克服するでしょう。私たちの生活空間にはハナのような人びとが数多くいます。そのような人びとに頻繁に出会うことは多くなく、また仮に出会ったとしても彼らがそのような立場に置かれていることすら気づかないことが多いかもしれません。

　おそらくこの教材を通じて得るべき最も重要なメッセージは、私たちがメディアを通じて得る情報やイメージ、さらには私たちが日常で接する他者や現象に対して、私たち自らが自己省察的な姿勢を持たなければいけないということでしょう。もしも本教材を通じて読者たちが、以前には気づくことのなかったことに気づいてくださるのであれば、より平和的で良い社会の一歩につながると信じます。

　本書は3人の執筆者によって手がけられた共同の成果であります。そして本書を作成する上でリ・ハナさんの協力を得ました。また、彼女が執筆した『日本に暮らす北朝鮮人、リ・ハナの一歩一歩』は多くのインスピレーションを与えてくれました。執筆者一同は本書の制作において、構想、執筆、編集、校正、翻訳、挿絵作成などの諸活動において協力してくださった、アジアプレスの石丸次郎さん、イラストレーターのチョン・インキョン先生、サンドラ・ファヒ先生、サム・マクドナルドさん、ジェレミー・トマス先生、青柳克幸さん、林眞理子さん、メリサンダ・ベルコウィッツ先生、クリスティーン・ベルさん、宋銀庭さんをはじめ、多くの方々にお世話になりました。この場を借りて心から御礼申し上げます。

オーストラリア国立大学・博士課程　マーカス・ベル

●編著者・イラストレーター略歴

金敬黙　キム・ギョンムク
現在、中京大学・国際教養学部で教鞭をとる。韓国外国語大学を卒業し、東京大学大学院総合文化研究科（国際社会科学専攻）で学んだ（博士、東京大学）。国際関係論、平和研究が専門分野である。最近は脱北者の海外移住をとりまくトランスナショナル・ネットワークやアジア太平洋地域の人の移住に関する研究に取り組んでいる。

マーカス・ベル　Markus Bell
現在、オーストラリア国立大学・アジア太平洋研究科の博士後期課程に在籍している。専門は移民、難民、アイデンティティや記憶に関するものであり、これらの分野の幅広い著述がある。<mpsbell@gmail.com> を通じて連絡が取れる。

スーザン・メナデュー・チョン　Susan Menadue-Chun
立教大学・大学院博士後期課程に在籍している。朝鮮学校の教員と総連系コミュニティのアイデンティティ変化についての研究に取り組んでいる。大学院での研究の傍ら、龍谷大学の安重根東洋平和センターで研究員を務める。

鄭仁敬　チョン・インキョン　Chung In-kyung
マンガ家。現在、東京工芸大学マンガ学科の助教である。1996 年に韓国で淑明女子大学・史学科を卒業し、2006 年月に京都精華大学大学院を修了した。個人ウェブサイト <http://chunginkyung.com>。

日英対訳・バイリンガル平和教育教材
私、北朝鮮から来ました──ハナのストーリー
Japanese-English, Bilingual Textbook for Peace Education
A North Korean Refugee in Japan—Hana's Stories

発行日	2016年1月1日 第1刷発行
編著者	金敬黙（キム・ギョンムク）
	マーカス・ベル（Markus Bell）
	スーザン・メナデュー・チョン（Susan Menadue-Chun）
発行者	石丸次郎
イラスト	チョン・インキョン
装丁・デザイン	林眞理子
発行・発売	アジアプレス・インターナショナル出版部
	〒530-0021 大阪市北区浮田1-2-3 サヌカイトビル303号
編集・販売	電話＋FAX 06-6224-3226
	Email　osaka@asiapress.org
	URL　http://asiapress.org/apn/

ISBN：978-4-904399-11-8
定価：本体 **1,270** 円＋税

乱丁落丁本は、お手数ですが小社販売部までお送りください。

本誌の写真・図表・原稿の無断転載を禁じます。
本誌の無断複写は、著作権法上の例外を除き、禁じられています。